BON APPÉTIT®

FAVORITES!

NEW FOR THE '90s

VOLUME TWO

BON APPETIT PUBLISHING CORP.
PUBLISHER

LOS ANGELES

INTRODUCTION

"What's cooking?"

It isn't surprising that a phrase that started in the kitchen is used so widely in our culture to express interest in anything new or exciting. Who, after all, can resist the temptation to walk up to the stove or oven, lift the lid or open the door, and see what culinary delights await?

Here at *Bon Appétit* you might say that "What's cooking?" are the words we all live by. It is our business—and, we happily add, our great pleasure—to explore and report to our readers on the latest developments in the world of food.

That world has grown all the more exciting and intriguing in the 1990s. New and exotic cuisines from Asia, Latin America, the Caribbean, Africa, and the Middle East delight our palates.

Old World cuisines that we thought were familiar beguile us anew with their regional variations: Instead of eating Italian food, for example, we now opt for Tuscan or Sicilian, Venetian or Milanese. Supermarkets tempt us with an ever-growing range of high-quality ingredients from around the world and fresh produce in dazzling array. And cooks everywhere are rising to the challenge of the widespread interest in healthy eating, providing us with innovative recipes that, though lighter, never stint on flavor.

The more than one hundred recipes in this volume, and the many tips and hints that accompany them, reflect all these trends, bringing you the very best from recent issues of *Bon Appétit*. And they point the way to many more exciting years of good eating to come as we approach the twenty-first century.

On the cover: Orange- and Basil-marinated Swordfish
Photograph by Ann Mitchell

BON APPÉTIT®

FAVORITES! NEW FOR THE '90s

VOLUME TWO

CONTENTS

continued on next page

Appetizers & Beverages

Today's cook has a world of options with which to begin a meal. Just witness the recipes that follow: from Asia, Baked Shrimp and Vegetable Spring Rolls; French-inspired Cold Poached Shrimp with Fennel Aioli; Moroccan-Style Eggplant Fritters; and refreshing drinks, from all-American Iced Spiced Lemonade to a trio of Caribbean punches. Best of all, a good appetite is all the passport you need!

Appetizers

SMOKED SALMON TARTARE

Since the flavor of this appetizer relies predominantly on the quality of salmon used, smoked salmon (not lox, which is soaked in a sugar brine and is saltier) is the best choice. You can purchase salmon trimmings at fish markets and at the fish counters of many supermarkets.

20 SERVINGS

SALMON

1½ pounds smoked salmon trimmings, chopped
½ cup finely chopped shallots or red onions
½ cup chopped fresh chives
2 tablespoons plus 2 teaspoons drained capers, coarsely chopped
2 tablespoons plus 2 teaspoons Dijon mustard
Cracked white pepper

CONDIMENTS

4 cucumbers
3 hard-boiled eggs, yolks and whites chopped separately
¾ cup sour cream
⅓ cup drained capers
⅓ cup chopped shallots or green onions
1 lemon, quartered, cut into thin slices

Fresh chives (garnish)
Toast points

FOR SALMON: Place first 5 ingredients in bowl. Season generously with white pepper. Using fork, stir to combine. Divide mixture in half. Form each half into thick patty. Wrap tightly in plastic and chill. (*Can be prepared 1 day ahead.*)

FOR CONDIMENTS: Thinly slice 1 cucumber. Overlap half of cucumber slices on platter in circle slightly larger than salmon patty. Repeat with remaining slices on another platter. Place 1 patty in center of each platter. Surround with chopped yolks and whites, sour cream, capers, shallots and lemon.

Garnish each salmon patty with chives. Cut remaining 3 cucumbers diagonally into thin slices. Serve salmon with cucumber slices and toast.

BAKED SHRIMP AND VEGETABLE SPRING ROLLS WITH HOISIN AND MUSTARD SAUCES

Spring rolls are among the best-known Chinese snacks. But for those watching their waistlines, they aren't the best choice on the menu because they're deep fried. Here's a recipe that bakes them instead, and the results are light, crisp and delicious. Choose fresh fruit, such as sliced melon, for a refreshing dessert.

MAKES 8 ROLLS

3 tablespoons dry sherry
3 tablespoons soy sauce
1 tablespoon minced garlic

1 tablespoon minced peeled fresh
   ginger
2 teaspoons Oriental sesame oil
2 teaspoons sugar
1 teaspoon cornstarch
¾ pound uncooked medium
   shrimp, peeled, deveined,
   coarsely chopped
1 cup thinly sliced red cabbage
1 cup ½-inch pieces snow peas
1 cup diced zucchini
1 cup diced red bell pepper
1 cup chopped green onions
3 tablespoons slivered almonds,
   toasted
3 tablespoons thinly sliced drained
   oil-packed sun-dried tomatoes

   Nonstick vegetable oil spray
4 sheets frozen phyllo dough,
   thawed and halved lengthwise
8 teaspoons vegetable oil mixed
   with 8 teaspoons water

   Lettuce leaves (garnish)
   Carrot julienne (garnish)

   Bell pepper julienne (garnish)
   Hoisin sauce
   Hot mustard sauce

Bring first 7 ingredients to boil in heavy
small saucepan, stirring constantly. Pour
into large bowl. Add shrimp, cabbage,
snow peas, zucchini, diced bell pepper,
green onions, almonds and sun-dried
tomatoes and toss well. (*Can be prepared
6 hours ahead. Cover and refrigerate.*)

   Preheat oven to 500°F. Spray heavy
large cookie sheet with nonstick vegetable
oil spray. Arrange 1 phyllo half-sheet (keep
remainder covered) on work surface.
Brush with 1½ teaspoons oil-water
mixture. Mound ⅔ cup filling at one short
end of phyllo, leaving 1-inch border on
sides. Roll phyllo over filling; fold in
sides. Continue rolling to enclose filling
completely. Transfer to prepared sheet.
Repeat with remaining phyllo and filling.
Brush spring rolls with remaining oil-
water mixture.

   Bake pastries until golden brown,
about 10 minutes. Divide spring rolls

among 4 plates. Garnish plates with
lettuce leaves, carrot and bell pepper
julienne. Serve, passing hoisin and hot
mustard sauces separately.

COLD POACHED SHRIMP WITH FENNEL AIOLI

*Shrimp and bell pepper strips are perfect
partners for the dipping sauce. If short on
time, purchase cooked shrimp.*

20 SERVINGS

AIOLI

2 medium fennel bulbs (about
   1½ pounds), roots trimmed
1½ cups plus 3 tablespoons olive oil
1½ teaspoons fennel seeds, chopped
1½ tablespoons white wine vinegar
   3 garlic cloves, sliced

   3 large egg yolks
   Salt
   White pepper

SHRIMP

2 carrots, chopped
2 teaspoons fennel seeds, crushed
2 teaspoons coriander seeds, crushed
2 cups dry white wine
2½ pounds uncooked medium
    shrimp, peeled, deveined (tails
    left intact), shells reserved
8 cups water

Yellow or red bell pepper strips
Fennel fronds or fresh dill sprigs
    (garnish)

FOR AIOLI: Cut stalks and fronds off fennel bulbs. Chop stalks and reserve stalks and fronds. Cut fennel bulbs into thin slices. Heat 3 tablespoons oil in heavy large skillet over medium heat. Add fennel slices, fennel seeds and vinegar. Sauté 10 minutes, stirring frequently; do not let color. Add 1½ garlic cloves and remaining oil. Reduce heat to low, cover and cook until fennel is tender, stirring occasionally, about 35 minutes.

Place remaining 1½ garlic cloves and yolks in blender. Add hot fennel using slotted spoon. Process until smooth. Gradually add oil from fennel mixture in slow steady stream. Process until emulsified. Season with salt and pepper. Return to skillet. Cook over low heat until aioli registers 160°F, whisking constantly, about 4 minutes. Cover and chill. (*Can be prepared 2 days ahead.*)

FOR SHRIMP: Place chopped carrots, crushed fennel seeds, crushed coriander seeds and dry white wine with reserved shrimp shells and reserved fennel stalks in heavy large pot. Add 8 cups water. Boil 25 minutes. Strain. Immediately return liquid to pot and add shrimp. Simmer until shrimp are opaque, about 2 minutes. Drain. Refresh shrimp in cold water and drain again. Cover and chill. (*Shrimp can be prepared 1 day ahead.*)

Transfer aioli to bowl. Place on platter. Drape shrimp around bowl rim. Arrange pepper strips on platter. Garnish aioli with fennel or fresh dill sprigs.

SMOKED CHICKEN AND GORGONZOLA IN ENDIVE SPEARS

MAKES 50

2 ounces green beans (preferably
    haricots verts)
8 ounces smoked chicken or smoked
    turkey, cut into ¼-inch dice
½ red bell pepper, cut into ¼-inch
    dice
⅓ cup watercress leaves, chopped
1 large shallot or green onion,
    minced
1 tablespoon chopped fresh tarragon
    or 1 teaspoon dried, crumbled

¼ cup walnut oil or olive oil
2 tablespoons white wine vinegar
¾ cup crumbled domestic
    Gorgonzola or other blue cheese
    (about 3 ounces)
3 tablespoons chopped toasted
    walnuts
Salt and pepper

4 Belgian endive heads, separated
   into spears
   Watercress leaves (garnish)

Bring small saucepan of water to boil.
Add green beans. Cook until just tender,
about 4 minutes. Drain. Refresh with cold
water and drain again. Thinly slice
crosswise. Combine with diced chicken,
diced red bell pepper, chopped watercress, minced shallot and tarragon in
medium bowl. (*Can be prepared 1 day
ahead. Cover and chill.*)

Place oil and vinegar in heavy small
saucepan. Bring mixture just to simmer,
swirling pan occasionally. Stir in
Gorgonzola cheese. Pour over salad
mixture. Toss to coat. Stir in toasted
walnuts. Season to taste with salt and
pepper. Cover and refrigerate at least
30 minutes or up to 8 hours.

Form 2 teaspoons salad into ball.
Press onto bottom portion of endive spear.
Repeat with remaining salad and endive.
Garnish each spear with watercress.

BUFFET PARTY PLANNER

Here are a few tips to help an afternoon or evening appetizer buffet go perfectly.

- Decide on a convenient location—or locations—to set up the buffet. Take a look at the "traffic flow" in your home. Maybe the dining room is not the best place for the food in this case. Or maybe you need to move the dining table so that people can help themselves more conveniently.

- It almost goes without saying that these days a "cocktail" party also means having on hand plenty of wine (for 20, plan on six bottles of white and four of red), Champagne (six bottles), two six-packs of beer and a selection of soft drinks, sparkling water and fruit juice.

- As far as the amount of liquor is concerned, plan on two bottles of whiskey and one bottle each of vodka and gin. If you know your guests' preferences, you might expand the selection with rum, vermouth, brandy, etc. Have mixers, lemons and limes available. And don't forget the ice.

ASTA'S BAKED-GARLIC APPETIZER

To eat, pierce a garlic clove; press to release from the skin and spread it on bread. Then top it with some of the melted cheese and sun-dried tomato mixture.

6 SERVINGS

4 large garlic heads, unpeeled
2½ tablespoons butter, thinly sliced
¼ cup olive oil
2 to 2½ cups canned chicken broth
2 cups sun-dried tomatoes
¾ tablespoon dried fines herbes
   Pepper

6 ounces goat cheese, sliced
   Fresh basil leaves (garnish)
1 large loaf Italian bread, sliced

Preheat oven to 375°F. Slice ¼ inch off tops of garlic heads (opposite root end). Remove any loose outer papery skin. Place garlic cut side up in medium baking dish. Arrange butter slices evenly over garlic. Pour oil over. Add 2 cups broth to dish.

Arrange sun-dried tomatoes around garlic. Sprinkle fines herbes over. Season with pepper. Bake until garlic and sun-dried tomatoes are tender, basting with broth every 15 minutes and adding more broth if necessary to maintain some sauce in pan, about 1 hour 15 minutes.

Arrange goat cheese around garlic and continue baking until cheese is almost melted, about 10 minutes. Garnish with basil. Serve with Italian bread.

TOMATO AND ARTICHOKE TORTE WITH PARMESAN CHEESE

To make this dish even easier, substitute a ten-ounce package of thawed frozen artichoke hearts for the freshly cooked. Terrific as a prelude to roast chicken.

6 SERVINGS

1 tablespoon lemon juice
1 tablespoon olive oil
4 large artichokes

1 cup chicken stock or canned
   broth
¾ pound russet potatoes, peeled,
   cut into ¾-inch dice
4 tablespoons (½ stick) unsalted
   butter
4 garlic cloves, coarsely chopped
1¼ cups freshly grated Parmesan
   cheese (about 5 ounces)
2 eggs
½ teaspoon dried thyme, crumbled
   Salt and pepper

2 tablespoons dry breadcrumbs
2 large tomatoes, peeled, seeded,
   thinly sliced, well drained

Bring medium pot of water to boil. Add lemon juice and oil. Reduce heat to medium. Add artichokes and cook until leaves pull away easily, about 40 minutes. Drain and cool. Peel off leaves. Scoop out chokes with spoon and discard, reserving hearts.

Bring stock to boil in heavy medium saucepan. Add potatoes. Cover and cook over medium-high heat until just tender, about 10 minutes. Drain potatoes. Transfer to processor.

Melt 2 tablespoons butter in heavy large skillet over medium heat. Add artichoke hearts and garlic and sauté 3 minutes. Add to potatoes in processor and coarsely purée. Transfer to bowl. Mix in 1 cup cheese, eggs, thyme, salt and pepper. *(Can be prepared 1 day ahead. Cover and refrigerate.)*

Preheat oven to 400°F. Butter 8-inch square baking dish. Coat with breadcrumbs. Transfer artichoke purée to prepared dish. Smooth top. Arrange tomato slices over. Cut remaining 2 tablespoons butter into small pieces and dot over surface. Sprinkle with remaining ¼ cup cheese. Bake torte until set and top is golden, about 35 minutes. Serve hot or at room temperature.

MOROCCAN-STYLE EGGPLANT FRITTERS

Cool the spicy flavors of the fritters with the Cilantro-Mint Yogurt dipping sauce. A delectable hors d'oeuvre.

MAKES ABOUT 12

1 large eggplant, peeled, cut into 2-inch pieces

2 large eggs
2 cups dry breadcrumbs
1 cup coarsely chopped fresh cilantro
½ cup golden raisins
½ cup plain yogurt
3 garlic cloves, finely chopped
½ jalapeño chili, finely chopped
2 teaspoons tomato paste
1 teaspoon Hungarian hot paprika
1 teaspoon ground cumin
½ teaspoon curry powder
½ teaspoon ground coriander
½ teaspoon salt
¼ teaspoon ground ginger

Pinch of ground cardamom
1 cup all purpose flour
2 eggs, beaten to blend

Vegetable oil (for frying)
Cilantro-Mint Yogurt (see recipe)
1 lime or lemon, cut into wedges

Place eggplant in top of vegetable steamer over boiling water. Cover and steam until tender, about 10 minutes. Drain well. Transfer to processor and purée. Place in fine sieve over bowl; drain 30 minutes.

Whisk eggplant purée, 2 eggs, 1 cup breadcrumbs and next 13 ingredients in large bowl (mixture will be very soft). Place 1 mounded tablespoon mixture into flour. Roll gently to coat. Dip into beaten eggs, then in remaining 1 cup breadcrumbs, coating completely. Flatten between palms of hands into 3-inch-long oval patty. Transfer to baking sheet. Repeat with remaining eggplant, flour, eggs and breadcrumbs.

Heat 3 inches oil in heavy large saucepan to 375°F. Add patties in batches and cook until golden brown, about 3 minutes per side. Transfer to paper towels using slotted spatula and drain. (*Can be prepared 2 hours ahead. Let stand at room temperature.*) Transfer fritters to plates. Serve hot or at room temperature with Cilantro-Mint Yogurt and lime or lemon.

CILANTRO-MINT YOGURT

MAKES ABOUT 1 CUP

1 cup plain yogurt
1 tablespoon coarsely chopped
   fresh mint leaves
1 tablespoon coarsely chopped
   fresh cilantro
1 teaspoon grated peeled fresh
   ginger
1 garlic clove, finely chopped
   Salt

Mix all ingredients in bowl. (*Can be prepared 8 hours ahead; chill.*)

TRICKS WITH TOMATOES

To peel tomatoes, stick a fork into the stem end, immerse the tomato in boiling water for 10 seconds and remove. Starting at the top, peel with a paring knife. The skin will slip off.

After hollowing a tomato for stuffing, turn it upside down to drain for a few hours. This prevents the tomato liquid from diluting the flavor of the filling. Sprinkle with salt and pepper and fill as desired. For baking, put the stuffed tomatoes in lightly oiled cupcake tins. The cups hold the tomatoes upright and help retain their rounded shape.

When a dish such as a fine sauce calls for juiced and seeded tomatoes, cut tomatoes in half widthwise. Press gently to squeeze out seeds and juice.

Cherry tomatoes may seem perfect for skewering and grilling, but their skins are tough and they get watery inside when heated. Use the larger firm, ripe tomatoes, stem ends removed. Cut each tomato in half widthwise and insert two bamboo skewers in each half. The double skewers hold the tomatoes firmly when they are turned on the grill.

EGGPLANT AND GORGONZOLA CROSTINI

For a terrific appetizer, slices of Italian bread are spread with prepared pesto and seasoned eggplant, then topped with Gorgonzola and provolone and broiled.

MAKES 14 TO 16

1 eggplant, peeled, diced
1 teaspoon salt

3 teaspoons olive oil
1 tablespoon minced garlic
1 tablespoon dried basil, crumbled
Pepper

½ cup prepared pesto sauce
1 8-ounce loaf Italian bread, sliced
4 ounces provolone cheese, grated
2 ounces Gorgonzola cheese, crumbled
Fresh basil leaves (garnish)

Spread eggplant on paper towel. Sprinkle with salt. Let stand 30 minutes to drain. Pat eggplant dry with paper towels.

Heat oil in heavy large skillet over medium-high heat. Add eggplant, garlic and dried basil and sauté until eggplant is tender and beginning to brown, 8 to 10 minutes. Season with pepper. (*Can be prepared 1 day ahead. Cover and refrigerate. Reheat before using.*)

Preheat broiler. Spread 1½ teaspoons pesto sauce over one side of each bread slice. Top each with 1 tablespoon eggplant mixture, then with 1 tablespoon provolone and ½ tablespoon Gorgonzola. Place on cookie sheet. Broil until cheese melts, 3 to 4 minutes. Garnish with fresh basil.

THYME-SCENTED GARLIC CUSTARDS

These first-course custards are rich and smooth, accented by mild garlic.

6 SERVINGS

30 garlic cloves (unpeeled)

1 tablespoon unsalted butter

1 tablespoon all purpose flour
2 cups chicken stock or canned low-salt broth
¼ teaspoon dried thyme, crumbled
Pepper

3 eggs
1 cup whipping cream
¾ cup freshly grated Parmesan cheese (about 3 ounces)
1 garlic clove, finely chopped

Bring medium saucepan of water to boil. Add unpeeled garlic and cook 1 minute. Drain well. Slip off skins.

Melt butter in heavy medium saucepan over medium-low heat. Add flour and stir until very light brown, about 3 minutes. Remove from heat. Gradually add stock, whisking until smooth. Cook over medium heat until sauce boils and thickens slightly, stirring frequently, about 5 minutes. Add 30 whole garlic cloves. Increase heat to medium-high and cook until garlic is tender and sauce is reduced to about 1¼ cups, stirring frequently, about 10 minutes. Add thyme and pepper.

Preheat oven to 300°F. Whisk eggs in large bowl with cream, Parmesan and 1 chopped garlic clove. Gradually whisk in hot garlic sauce. Pour custard into six ½-cup soufflé dishes or custard cups, dividing garlic cloves evenly. Place dishes in large baking pan. Add enough hot water to pan to come halfway up sides of dishes. Bake until custards are just set, about 30 minutes. Remove custards from water bath. Serve warm or at room temperature. *(Can be prepared 2 hours ahead.)*

White Bean Dip with Chips and Sticks

A new twist on the usual bean dip.

12 SERVINGS

3 garlic cloves
3 15-ounce cans cannellini (white kidney beans), rinsed, drained
¼ cup fresh lemon juice
½ cup olive oil
2¼ teaspoons ground cumin
1½ teaspoons chili powder
   Salt and freshly ground pepper
3 tablespoons minced fresh cilantro
   Additional minced fresh cilantro
   Fresh vegetables (such as carrot sticks, celery sticks and cauliflower)
   Tortilla chips

Finely chop garlic in processor. Add beans and lemon juice and purée. Mix in oil, cumin and chili powder. Season with salt and pepper. Add 3 tablespoons cilantro and mix in using on/off turns. Transfer to large bowl. *(Can be prepared 1 day ahead. Cover and refrigerate.)* Sprinkle dip with cilantro. Serve with vegetables and chips.

Cold Bell Peppers Stuffed with Ricotta Cheese and Herbs

You can stuff and bake the peppers the day before. Serve them whole or cut crosswise into ½-inch-thick slices and fan them on plates. Try to purchase peppers with flat, even bottoms so they will stand upright during baking. Serve as an appetizer to a grilled chicken or fish dinner.

6 SERVINGS

PEPPERS

3 medium-size yellow bell peppers
3 medium-size red bell peppers

3 cups whole-milk ricotta cheese
2 eggs
⅓ cup freshly grated Parmesan cheese
3 garlic cloves, finely chopped
1 teaspoon chopped fresh rosemary or ¼ teaspoon dried, crumbled
   Salt and pepper

DRESSING

4 garlic cloves, minced
3 tablespoons red wine vinegar
1 tablespoon Dijon mustard
1 tablespoon tomato paste
½ cup plus 1 tablespoon olive oil
    Salt and pepper

⅓ cup coarsely chopped fresh basil
    Kalamata olives* (garnish)

FOR PEPPERS: Lightly oil 9x13-inch baking dish. Char peppers over gas flame or in broiler until blackened in several spots on all sides. Wrap in plastic bag and let stand 20 minutes to steam. Peel charred skin off peppers. Rinse peppers under running water. Cut 1 inch off peppers at stem end. Remove seeds. Pat peppers dry with paper towels. Arrange peppers cut side up in prepared baking dish.

Preheat oven to 325°F. Mix ricotta, eggs, Parmesan, garlic and rosemary in medium bowl. Season with salt and pepper. Spoon stuffing into peppers. Bake until filling begins to set and tops are just crusty, about 35 minutes. Cool, then cover and refrigerate at least 4 hours. (Can be prepared 1 day ahead.)

FOR DRESSING: Whisk garlic, vinegar, mustard and tomato paste in bowl. Gradually whisk in oil. Season with salt and pepper. (Can be prepared 1 day ahead. Store at room temperature.)

Arrange peppers on platter. Mix basil into dressing and spoon over peppers. Garnish with olives and serve.

Black brine-cured Kalamata olives are available at Greek and Italian markets and some supermarkets.

GARLICKY EGGPLANT SPREAD

8 SERVINGS

2 large eggplants (about
    2½ pounds)
2 large garlic cloves, slivered

¼ cup olive oil
2 tablespoons fresh lemon juice
2 tablespoons chopped fresh oregano or 2 teaspoons dried, crumbled
1 teaspoon ground cumin
    Salt and pepper

    Red leaf lettuce
4 tomatoes, sliced
    Pita bread
    Chopped fresh oregano

Preheat oven to 450°F. Cut slits in eggplants with tip of knife and insert garlic sliver into each slit. Place eggplants in baking pan and bake until very tender, about 1 hour. Cut each eggplant in half and cool slightly.

Scrape eggplant pulp from skin into colander and let drain. Transfer eggplant to processor. Add oil, lemon juice, 2 tablespoons oregano and cumin. Purée until smooth. Season with salt and pepper. Cool completely. (Can be prepared 1 day ahead. Cover and refrigerate.)

Line platter with lettuce. Halve tomato slices and arrange around edge of platter. Cut pita into wedges and arrange around platter. Mound eggplant mixture in center. Sprinkle with oregano.

Beverages

TROPICAL FRUIT AND RUM PUNCH

12 SERVINGS

2 12-ounce cans mango nectar
2 12-ounce cans guava nectar
2 cups canned unsweetened
   pineapple juice
1½ cups canned coconut cream
   (such as Coco Lopez), well mixed
¼ cup fresh lime juice
2 cups amber (gold) rum

17 cups ice cubes
   Fresh pineapple or lime wedges
   (garnish)

Combine mango nectar, guava nectar, pineapple juice, coconut cream, lime juice and amber rum in large pitcher. *(Punch can be prepared 1 day ahead. Cover and refrigerate. Mix well before using.)*

Combine 1 cup punch and 2 cups ice cubes in blender and blend until smooth and thick. Pour into glasses. Garnish with fresh pineapple or lime wedges and serve. Repeat with remaining punch in batches.

ICED SPICED LEMONADE

Honey and spices update a classic lemonade. Also have Champagne on hand.

MAKES ABOUT 32 CUPS

8 lemons
32 cups water (8 quarts)
40 whole cloves
1 tablespoon cardamom pods
2 cups honey

   Ice cubes
   Lemon slices (garnish)

Cut lemons in half and juice; reserve shells. Bring water to boil in large pot. Remove from heat. Add lemon juice and lemon shells, cloves and cardamom to water. Cover and let stand 20 minutes.

Add honey and stir to dissolve. Strain lemonade through sieve into pitchers. Chill until very cold, at least 3 hours. *(Can be prepared 1 day ahead.)*

Fill tall glasses with ice cubes. Pour spiced lemonade over. Garnish with lemon slices and serve.

FIZZY AND FATTENING?

SELTZERS AND SPARKLING MINERAL waters are great coolers—but while you're sipping, are calories sneaking up on you? Although a variety of flavored sparklers are calorie-free, many are not, according to the *University of California, Berkeley, Wellness Letter.* The publishers say to watch out for those beverages with added sweeteners that can increase calorie counts to match those of regular colas. Look for drinks labeled "calorie-free" or, better still, "calorie- and salt-free."

PETIT PUNCH

Petit Punch—little punch—is the West Indian version of a martini. The term punch *comes from the Hindi word for five, because it was traditionally made from five ingredients: lime, water, sugar, spices and spirits. According to Michel Ledée, owner of the Marigot Bay Club on St. Barts, this drink is called "right punch" when made with white rum, and "left punch" when made with dark rum. For best results, use a rum like Rhum St. James or Rhum Clément from Martinique. Sip this straight up, as the locals do, or if you prefer, try it on the rocks.*

2 SERVINGS

¼ cup plus 2 tablespoons white
   or dark rum
2 tablespoons Citrus Sugar Syrup
   (see recipe)
6 ice cubes
2 lime wedges

Combine rum and syrup in small pitcher or martini shaker. Add ice cubes and stir. Strain mixture into 2 chilled martini glasses. Squeeze lime wedge into each and serve.

MANGO DAIQUIRI

The daiquiri originated in Cuba at the turn of the century. It is named for the iron mines in the town of Daiquirí near Santiago. The drink was christened by the American engineers who worked there after the Spanish-American War. Today, daiquiris are made with a variety of fruits and served all over the Caribbean. This unusual version comes from Hubert Delamotte, owner of the lovely Hostellerie des Trois Forces on St. Barts. Be sure to use very ripe mangoes.

4 SERVINGS

¼ cup sugar
4 lime slices

2 large ripe mangoes, peeled, pitted,
   chopped
2 cups crushed ice
¾ cup light rum
½ cup Citrus Sugar Syrup (see recipe)
½ cup soda water

4 hibiscus blossoms (optional
   garnish)

Place sugar on small plate. Rub rims of four 8-ounce glasses with lime slices; reserve limes. Dip glasses into sugar.

   Combine mangoes, ice, rum, syrup and soda water in blender. Purée until smooth. Divide mixture among glasses. Garnish each with one reserved lime slice and optional blossom.

CITRUS SUGAR SYRUP

MAKES ABOUT 1½ CUPS

1 cup water
1 cup sugar
4 ½x2-inch pieces lemon peel
   (yellow part only)
2 tablespoons fresh lime juice

Bring first 3 ingredients to boil in heavy small saucepan, stirring until sugar dissolves. Cool completely. Strain into jar. Stir in lime juice. (*Can be prepared 1 month ahead. Cover jar and refrigerate.*)

RUM: THE STRAIGHT FACTS

PRODUCTION METHODS

Most rum is made from molasses, but in Guadeloupe and Martinique the spirit is also distilled directly from fresh sugar cane juice. Distillation usually takes place in industrial continuous stills; a few brands, like Haiti's Rhum Barbancourt, use the traditional pear-shaped copper pot still of the sort used in Scotland and in the Cognac region of France. Jamaicans favor "dunder" rums, made like sour mash in Kentucky. (Dunder is a portion of fermented molasses held back from the distillation and added to subsequent batches of mash.) Dunder adds a rich flavor to rum, much the way a sourdough starter flavors bread. This type of rum is known as "plummer" in Jamaica and as *grand arôme* in the French West Indies.

BLENDING AND AGING

Rum acquires its seductive taste through an elaborate process of blending and aging. The aging process can be as short as 12 months for white rum or as long as 15 years for an estate reserve. Distillers generally age their product in oak barrels but it is speculated that some use such flavor enhancers as old sherry casks and bourbon barrels. The gold and dark rums are generally colored with caramel. Most rums are a combination of younger and older spirits, and the better ones will have a minimum age of 4 to 5 years.

DIFFERENT TYPES

White rum (also called silver rum) is the most highly refined and mildest in flavor. Gold rum (also called amber rum) has a richer, fuller flavor and is excellent for sipping with tonic. Dark rums possess the fullest flavor and are excellent for mixing with fruit juices. There is even a 151-proof rum, sometimes called "overproof," which is used for cooking.

BUBBLY GRAMMAR

Named for the region in northern France from which it hails, Champagne was "invented" about three hundred years ago when a Benedictine monk named Dom Pérignon began blending grapes from different varieties and vineyards to create a wine more subtle than any of its parts. He then discovered how to keep the wine's natural sparkle—by inducing a second fermentation in a tightly corked bottle. Involving a process that took a century of trial and error, the bubbles are caused by carbon dioxide that has been dissolved in the wine.

Today, of course, Champagne is the beverage of choice at most celebrations. In order to select the one that appeals to you most and that is most appropriate to your menu, it is helpful to have an understanding of the terms used by Champagne bottlers.

Brut, Extra Dry: Indicates level of sweetness. In order to control the amount of sugar in a finished wine, it is usually topped off with a mixture of wine, sugar and sometimes brandy. Brut is the drier of the two. Some producers also make an ultra brut, which is completely dry.

Nonvintage (NV): The *cuvée* or "house blend," which is the secret patent and signature wine of each Champagne house. It remains standard year after year and is usually released to the market for sale when very young.

Vintage: Wine that is considered too fine to be blended with the nonvintage cuvée. As a result, it is aged longer to produce a fuller-bodied wine.

Blanc de Blancs: A blend of Chardonnay grapes only; this wine is lighter than traditional Champagne.

Blanc de Noirs: A rich and dense white Champagne that comes from a cuvée of black grapes exclusively.

Crémant: Only half as bubbly as normal; often preferred with food.

Cuvée de Prestige: The best that a Champagne house has to offer; also, usually their most costly wine. Also called *tête de cuvée*.

Rosé: Pink Champagne that is blended with a small amount of still red wine, typically Pinot Noir. It is a little bit fruitier than white Champagne and often the most interesting cuvée available from a house.

Soups & Salads

Recent years have witnessed a revolution in soups and salads. As intensely satisfying as soups have always been, recipes such as Gingered Fish and Watercress Soup and Chilled Summer Squash Soup with Curry now benefit from exotic seasonings and healthier, more stream-lined ingredients. And dazzling salads such as Tropical Chicken and Duck and Cantaloupe provide a deliciously light and refreshing alter-native to weightier main-course fare.

Soups

GARLIC AND SAFFRON SOUP

4 SERVINGS

5 tablespoons olive oil
2 cups trimmed sourdough bread
  cubes
4 large garlic cloves, quartered
⅓ cup dry white wine
4 cups canned low-salt chicken
  broth
2 generous pinches saffron threads

Salt
8 ½-inch-thick French bread
  baguette slices
½ cup grated Manchego* or
  Monterey Jack cheese
  Minced fresh chives or green
  onion tops
  Saffron threads

Heat 4 tablespoons oil in heavy large skillet over medium-high heat. Add bread cubes and garlic and sauté until bread is light golden, about 4 minutes. Add wine, then broth and saffron; bring to boil. Reduce heat, cover and simmer 25 minutes. Purée soup in blender. Return soup to saucepan. Season with salt.

Preheat oven to 350°F. Arrange bread slices on cookie sheet. Brush with remaining 1 tablespoon oil. Bake until lightly toasted, about 8 minutes. Sprinkle cheese over croutons. Transfer cookie sheet to broiler; broil until cheese melts. Place 2 croutons in each bowl. Bring soup to simmer. Ladle over croutons. Sprinkle with chives and a few saffron threads and serve.

A Spanish sheep's-milk cheese available at some cheese shops, Spanish markets and specialty foods stores.

GINGERED FISH AND WATERCRESS SOUP

4 SERVINGS

½ ounce dried Chinese black
  mushrooms or dried shiitake
  mushrooms
½ cup hot water

1½ teaspoons peanut oil
1 teaspoon Oriental sesame oil
3 green onions, minced
2 large garlic cloves, minced
1 tablespoon plus 1 teaspoon
  minced, peeled fresh ginger
3 cups canned low-salt chicken
  broth
¼ cup bottled clam juice
1 tablespoon dry sherry
1 tablespoon soy sauce
½ pound catfish or other white-flesh
  fish fillets, cut into ¾-inch cubes
3 large bunches watercress,
  trimmed

Soak mushrooms in ½ cup hot water until softened, about 20 minutes. Drain mushrooms, reserving soaking liquid. Squeeze out excess moisture. Thinly slice caps, discarding stems.

Heat peanut oil and sesame oil in heavy large saucepan over medium heat. Add green onions, garlic and ginger and sauté until just tender, about 3 minutes. Add sliced mushrooms and sauté until mushrooms are tender, about 3 minutes. Add chicken broth, mushroom soaking liquid, clam juice, sherry and soy sauce. Bring to boil. Stir in catfish and watercress and boil until fish is just cooked through, about 2 minutes.

CREAM OF RATATOUILLE SOUP

4 SERVINGS

3 tablespoons olive oil
1 eggplant, peeled, chopped
1 large onion, coarsely chopped
1 large red bell pepper, chopped
1 medium zucchini, chopped
2 large garlic cloves, minced
2 large tomatoes, coarsely chopped
2 tablespoons chopped fresh thyme or 2 teaspoons dried, crumbled

¾ cup (or more) chicken stock or canned broth
¼ cup whipping cream
Salt and pepper
Croutons

Heat 2 tablespoons olive oil in heavy large deep skillet over medium heat. Add eggplant, onion, bell pepper, zucchini and garlic and cook until just soft, stirring occasionally, about 15 minutes. Add remaining 1 tablespoon olive oil, tomatoes and thyme. Reduce heat to medium-low, cover and cook until vegetables are very tender, stirring occasionally, about 20 minutes.

Processing in batches, purée vegetable mixture in blender with ¾ cup stock. Transfer purée to saucepan. Add cream. Season with salt and pepper. (Can be prepared 1 day ahead. Cover and chill.) Cook until soup is heated through, about 5 minutes, thinning with additional stock if desired. Ladle into bowls. Sprinkle with croutons.

BARLEY AND LENTIL SOUP

8 SERVINGS

3 tablespoons olive oil
2 large onions, chopped
4 garlic cloves, chopped
3 carrots, sliced
4 celery stalks, chopped
1 red bell pepper, chopped
8 oil-packed sun-dried tomatoes, drained, chopped
2 teaspoons dried basil, crumbled
1 teaspoon dried oregano, crumbled

6 14¼-ounce cans (about) beef broth
1 28-ounce can crushed tomatoes
2 tablespoons tomato paste
1 cup pearl barley

1 cup lentils

Salt and pepper
¼ cup chopped fresh parsley
(optional garnish)

Heat oil in heavy 4-quart saucepan over medium-high heat. Add onions and garlic and sauté until onions are translucent, about 10 minutes. Add next 6 ingredients. Cook until bell pepper just softens, stirring occasionally, 6 minutes.

Mix in 5 cans broth, tomatoes and tomato paste. Bring mixture to boil. Stir in barley and lentils. Reduce heat and simmer until barley and lentils are tender, stirring occasionally, about 1½ hours.

Thin soup to desired consistency with remaining broth. Season with salt and pepper. Ladle into soup bowls and garnish with parsley if desired.

GINGER-CARROT BISQUE

A ladleful of this rich yet delicate soup is a delightful way to begin the feast. Certain spices, like ginger, were highly prized by the early colonists because their flavors evoked memories of favorite holiday dishes from England.

10 SERVINGS

¼ cup plus 2 tablespoons unsalted
  butter
2 pounds carrots, peeled, thinly
  sliced
2 large onions, chopped
1 tablespoon minced peeled fresh
  ginger
2 teaspoons grated orange peel
½ teaspoon ground coriander
5 cups chicken stock or canned
  broth
1 cup half-and-half
  Salt and pepper
½ cup minced fresh parsley

Melt butter in heavy large saucepan over medium heat. Add carrots and onions.

Cover saucepan and cook until vegetables begin to soften, stirring occasionally, about 15 minutes. Mix in ginger, orange peel and coriander. Add 2 cups stock. Reduce heat to medium-low. Cover pan and simmer soup until carrots are very tender, about 30 minutes. Purée soup in batches in processor or blender. Add remaining 3 cups stock and half-and-half to soup. Season with salt and pepper. (*Can be prepared 1 day ahead. Cover and refrigerate.*) Cook over medium heat until warm. Ladle into bowls. Sprinkle with parsley and serve.

SPINACH AND LENTIL SOUP

6 SERVINGS

5 cups (about) canned beef broth
1 cup lentils

2 tablespoons olive oil
1 large onion, chopped
1 small green bell pepper, chopped
1 celery stalk, chopped

1 8-ounce can tomato sauce
¼ cup purchased salsa
1 10-ounce package frozen chopped
   spinach, thawed, drained
   Salt and pepper

Bring 4 cups broth and lentils to boil in large saucepan. Simmer until lentils are just tender, about 30 minutes.

Meanwhile, heat olive oil in heavy large skillet over medium-high heat. Add onion, bell pepper and celery and sauté until tender, about 10 minutes.

Add onion mixture to lentils. Stir in tomato sauce and salsa. Simmer over medium-low heat until lentils are very tender, about 30 minutes. Thin soup with additional broth if necessary. Stir in spinach and simmer until heated through, about 2 minutes. Season soup to taste with salt and pepper.

COOL-AS-A-CUCUMBER POTATO AND MINT SOUP

Serve in mugs along with sandwiches.

6 SERVINGS

¼ cup (½ stick) unsalted butter
1 large onion, chopped
4 large cucumbers (about 2¾
   pounds), peeled, seeded, chopped
1 pound boiling potatoes, peeled,
   chopped
4 cups chicken stock or canned
   broth

½ cup plus 2 tablespoons
   half-and-half
¼ cup finely chopped fresh mint
3 tablespoons red wine vinegar
½ teaspoon freshly ground white
   pepper
   Salt
   Fresh mint sprigs (garnish)

Melt butter in heavy large saucepan over low heat. Add onion; cover and cook until translucent, stirring occa-sionally, about 15 minutes. Increase heat to high. Add cucumbers, potatoes and stock and bring to boil. Reduce heat, cover and simmer until potatoes are tender, about 30 minutes. Cool. Purée soup in batches in blender or processor until smooth. Strain soup into large bowl. Cover and refrigerate until well chilled, about 8 hours.

Stir half-and-half, chopped mint, red wine vinegar and white pepper into soup. Season with salt. (*Can be prepared 1 day ahead. Cover and refrigerate.*) Ladle soup into mugs. Garnish with mint sprigs and serve.

CHILLED SUMMER SQUASH SOUP WITH CURRY

This soup is also delicious served hot.

4 SERVINGS

2 tablespoons (¼ stick) unsalted
   butter
2 large shallots, minced

1 garlic clove, minced
1½ teaspoons curry powder
1¼ pounds yellow crookneck squash,
  diced
2 cups (or more) chicken stock or
  canned broth
  Salt
  Plain yogurt
  Minced fresh mint leaves
  (garnish)

Melt butter in heavy large saucepan over medium-low heat. Add shallots, garlic and curry and sauté 3 minutes. Add squash, cover and cook until squash is tender, stirring occasionally, about 10 minutes. Add 2 cups stock, cover and simmer 10 minutes. Purée in batches in blender or processor. Cover and chill until cold. (*Can be prepared 1 day ahead.*) Thin with additional stock, if necessary. Season with salt. Ladle into bowls. Top with dollop of yogurt. Garnish with mint.

Salads

LOBSTER SALAD WITH GREEN BEANS, CORN AND BELL PEPPER

Even easier, buy cooked lobster tails. Pour a Sauvignon Blanc or Fumé Blanc.

4 SERVINGS

SALAD

4 1½-pound live lobsters with claws
2 cups fresh green beans, cut into
  1-inch pieces
2 cups fresh corn kernels or frozen,
  thawed
1 large red bell pepper, cut into
  matchstick-size strips
¼ cup diced onion

DRESSING

3 tablespoons tarragon vinegar
3 teaspoons cracked black pepper
1½ tablespoons coarse-grained
  mustard

1 tablespoon honey
¾ cup vegetable oil
3 tablespoons finely chopped fresh
  tarragon or 2 teaspoons dried,
  crumbled

  Small butter lettuce leaves or
  lamb's lettuce (mâche) (garnish)
  Lemon wedges (garnish)

FOR SALAD: Cook lobsters in large pot of boiling water until bright red, about 12 minutes. Drain and cool. Crack shells; remove tail and claw meat in whole pieces. Cover and chill until ready to use. (*Can be prepared 1 day ahead.*)

Bring medium saucepan of salted water to boil. Add green beans and cook until just tender, about 2 minutes. Transfer to bowl of ice water using slotted spoon and cool. Return water to boil. Add corn kernels and cook until just tender, about 3 minutes. Drain. Transfer to bowl of ice water and cool. Drain green beans and corn. Transfer to large bowl. Add bell pepper and diced onion and set aside.

FOR DRESSING: Bring vinegar and pepper to simmer in heavy small saucepan. Whisk in mustard and honey. Gradually whisk in oil. Remove from heat. Mix in tarragon. Pour half of dressing over vegetables in bowl. Let stand 1 hour at room temperature.

Slice each lobster tail into medallions and fan on 1 side of each plate. Spoon vegetable salad in center of plates. Garnish with lettuce, claw meat and lemon wedges. Serve, passing remaining dressing separately.

TROPICAL CHICKEN SALAD

4 SERVINGS

4 boneless chicken breasts
  Salt and pepper

¼ cup olive oil
3 tablespoons red wine vinegar
1 teaspoon Dijon mustard
¼ teaspoon dried rubbed sage
6 cups salad greens

1 papaya, peeled, seeded, chopped
1 mango, peeled, pitted, chopped
1 6-ounce basket raspberries
1 tablespoon minced fresh mint
½ cup chopped toasted walnuts

Preheat oven to 425°F. Place chicken in baking pan. Season generously with salt and pepper. Bake until cooked through, about 20 minutes. Cool completely; cut chicken into bite-size pieces.

Whisk olive oil, vinegar, mustard and sage to blend in small bowl. Combine chicken, salad greens, papaya, mango, raspberries and mint in large bowl. Add dressing and toss well. Divide among 4 plates. Sprinkle with walnuts and serve.

BLACK BEAN AND RICE SALAD

12 SERVINGS

2 14½-ounce cans chicken broth
½ cup water
1 1-pound package long-grain rice
2 bay leaves

2 15-ounce cans black beans, drained, rinsed
2 red bell peppers, diced
1 green bell pepper, diced
1 medium red onion, diced
1 medium bunch fresh cilantro, chopped
½ cup olive oil
3 tablespoons orange juice
2 tablespoons red wine vinegar
2 teaspoons ground cumin
1 teaspoon chili powder
  Salt and pepper
  Lettuce leaves
  Fresh cilantro sprigs (garnish)

Bring chicken broth and water to boil in heavy large saucepan. Add rice and bay leaves. Bring to boil. Reduce heat to low, cover and cook until liquid is absorbed, about 20 minutes.

Transfer rice to large bowl and fluff with fork. Mix in black beans, bell peppers, red onion, chopped cilantro, oil, orange juice, vinegar, cumin and chili powder. Season to taste with salt and pepper. *(Can be prepared 1 day ahead. Cover and refrigerate.)* Line platter with lettuce. Mound salad on platter. Garnish with fresh cilantro sprigs and serve.

SPINACH AND BULGUR SALAD

Bulgur—cracked wheat—is a Middle Eastern staple that can be purchased at natural foods stores and in the natural foods sections of some supermarkets.

4 SERVINGS

½ cup bulgur
½ cup boiling water

1 cup plain yogurt
¼ cup olive oil
2 tablespoons red wine vinegar
2 garlic cloves, minced
1 teaspoon ground cumin
  Salt and pepper
8 cups fresh spinach leaves, torn
  into bite-size pieces
½ large red onion, sliced

½ cup sliced black olives
¼ cup freshly grated Parmesan

Combine bulgur and boiling water in small bowl. Let stand until bulgur has absorbed water, about 10 minutes. Cool bulgur completely.

For dressing, stir yogurt and next 4 ingredients in another small bowl. Season to taste with salt and pepper. Place spinach, onion, olives, Parmesan and bulgur in large bowl. Add enough dressing to season to taste. Toss well.

SPRING SALAD

A composed salad that features all the bright and pretty colors of the season.

6 SERVINGS

⅓ cup walnut oil or other nut oil
2 medium shallots, minced
2 tablespoons fresh pink grapefruit
  juice
¼ teaspoon sugar
  Salt
  White pepper

3 pink grapefruit
3 Belgian endive heads

1 head radicchio, thinly sliced
2 avocados, peeled, pitted
¼ cup chopped fresh chives
  Toasted chopped walnuts

Whisk first 4 ingredients together in small bowl. Season dressing to taste with salt and white pepper.

Using small sharp knife, remove peel and white pith from grapefruit. Working over large bowl to catch juice, cut between membranes to release segments. Squeeze juice from membranes into bowl. Reserve juice and segments separately. Trim bases from endive heads and separate into spears. *(Can be prepared 1 day ahead. Cover dressing, grapefruit, juice and endive separately and refrigerate.)*

Place sliced radicchio on platter. Arrange endive spears in rows atop radicchio. Thinly slice avocados. Dip avocado slices into reserved grapefruit juice. Fill each endive spear with 1 avocado slice and top with 1 grapefruit segment. Whisk chopped fresh chives into dressing and drizzle over salad. Sprinkle with toasted chopped walnuts.

SOUTHWEST TURKEY AND RICE SALAD

Instead of white rice, you can use brown rice, orzo (rice-shaped pasta) or any other small pasta. Serve hot flour tortillas with butter alongside the colorful salad, then finish with sliced summer fruit and a purchased angel food cake.

4 SERVINGS

1½ cups water
1 cup long-grain white rice
2 cups diced cooked turkey or chicken
¾ pound ripe plum tomatoes, seeded, diced
1 cup thinly sliced green bell pepper
1 cup corn kernels, cooked fresh or frozen, thawed
⅓ cup chopped red onion

½ cup olive oil
6 tablespoons chopped fresh cilantro
3 tablespoons white wine vinegar
1 tablespoon Dijon mustard
1 large jalapeño chili, seeded if desired, minced
1¼ teaspoons ground cumin
¾ teaspoon salt
¾ teaspoon pepper

Red leaf lettuce
1 ripe avocado, peeled, sliced

Bring 1½ cups water to boil in heavy medium saucepan. Mix in long-grain white rice. Cover and cook over low heat until rice is just tender, about 18 minutes. Transfer rice to large bowl. Add turkey, tomatoes, green bell pepper, corn and onion; toss.

Whisk together olive oil, cilantro, vinegar, mustard, chili, cumin, salt and pepper. Pour dressing over salad and mix gently. (*Can be prepared 3 hours ahead. Cover and refrigerate.*)

Arrange lettuce leaves on platter. Mound salad in center. Garnish with avocado slices and serve.

DUCK AND CANTALOUPE SALAD WITH CHUTNEY DRESSING

The sweetness of duck and melon are irresistible in this colorful dish, which is also delicious when made with dark turkey meat or chicken breasts. Offer warm, buttery croissants with the salad, then splurge on apple strudel from the bakery for dessert—served à la mode, of course.

4 SERVINGS

DRESSING

¾ cup peanut oil or vegetable oil
½ cup plus 1 tablespoon mango chutney
¼ cup plus 2 tablespoons white wine vinegar
1 tablespoon Dijon mustard
1 tablespoon soy sauce
1 tablespoon Oriental sesame oil

¾ teaspoon dried crushed red
pepper
2 large garlic cloves, chopped
Salt and pepper

SALAD

6 boneless duck breast halves
or 4 large boneless chicken breast
halves
2 tablespoons peanut oil or
vegetable oil

2 cups cantaloupe chunks (about
¾-inch pieces)
1 cup thinly sliced celery
½ cup thinly sliced green onions
⅓ cup roasted salted cashews
Lettuce leaves

FOR DRESSING: Pureé all ingredients in
processor or blender. Season to taste
with salt and pepper. (Can be prepared
1 day ahead. Cover and refrigerate.)

FOR SALAD: Generously salt and
pepper duck pieces. Heat oil in heavy
large skillet over medium-high heat.
Cook duck, skin side down, until very

brown and crisp, about 5 minutes. Turn
and sauté duck until just cooked through,
about 5 minutes longer. Transfer duck to
platter; cool slightly. Discard skin. Thinly
slice duck across grain.

Combine duck, cantaloupe and
celery in large bowl. Reserve 1 tablespoon
green onions and add remainder to salad.
(Can be prepared 4 hours ahead. Cover and
refrigerate.) Add cashews to salad. Toss with
enough dressing to coat. Arrange lettuce
leaves on plates. Mound salad on lettuce.
Sprinkle reserved green onions over. Serve,
passing remaining dressing separately.

GREEN VEGETABLE SALAD WITH ORANGE-HAZELNUT DRESSING

20 SERVINGS

SALAD

1½ pounds sugar snap peas,
stemmed, strings removed
1½ pounds green beans, cut into
1-inch-long pieces

2 large broccoli bunches, stemmed,
cut into florets
2 pounds asparagus, trimmed, cut
into 1-inch-long pieces

DRESSING

1½ cups olive oil (preferably
extra-virgin)
⅔ cup red wine vinegar
⅔ cup orange juice
2 tablespoons grated orange peel
½ teaspoon salt
¾ cup hazelnuts, toasted, finely
chopped

Peel (orange part only) from
1 orange, cut into thin strips
(garnish)

FOR SALAD: Bring large pot of salted water
to boil. Add sugar snap peas and cook
until bright green and crisp, about 1 minute. Using shotted spoon, transfer peas
to bowl of ice water and cool. Drain peas.
Return water in pot to boil. Add green
beans and cook until crisp-tender, about
5 minutes. Using slotted spoon, transfer

beans to bowl of ice water and cool. Drain beans. Return water in pot to boil. Add broccoli and asparagus and cook until crisp-tender, about 3 minutes. Drain well. Transfer to bowl of ice water and cool. Drain thoroughly. Combine all vegetables in large bowl. (*Can be prepared 1 day ahead. Cover and chill.*)

FOR DRESSING: Whisk first 5 ingredients in small bowl. Mix in hazelnuts.

Pour dressing over vegetables and toss gently. Garnish with orange peel strips and serve.

FRISÉE AND RADISH SALAD WITH GOAT CHEESE CROUTONS

Frisée is French for curly endive.

4 SERVINGS

  2 tablespoons sherry vinegar
  2 teaspoons Dijon mustard
  1 shallot or green onion, minced
  ⅓ cup olive oil

  Salt and pepper
  1 small head curly endive, torn into bite-size pieces
  1 bunch radishes, trimmed, thinly sliced
 12 ½-inch-thick slices French bread baguette
    Olive oil
  4 ounces soft fresh goat cheese (such as Montrachet)

Combine vinegar, mustard and shallot in small bowl. Whisk in ⅓ cup oil. Season dressing to taste with salt and pepper. Combine endive and radishes in large bowl. (*Can be prepared 4 hours ahead. Cover salad with damp towel and refrigerate. Cover dressing and let stand at room temperature.*)

Preheat broiler. Broil 1 side of bread until golden brown. Brush second side with olive oil. Season with salt and pepper. Spread with goat cheese. Season with pepper. Broil until bread is brown. Cut each slice into quarters.

Add dressing to salad and toss to coat. Divide among plates. Top with croutons and serve immediately.

MIXED GREENS WITH SAUTÉED MUSHROOMS AND LEEKS

4 SERVINGS

  ¼ cup hazelnut oil or olive oil
  ¾ pound shiitake, oyster or button mushrooms, halved
  1 cup sliced leeks (white part only)
  1 tablespoon fresh lemon juice
  1 garlic clove, minced
  1 tablespoon dry sherry
  1 tablespoon chopped fresh parsley
  1 teaspoon sherry wine vinegar
  1 teaspoon Dijon mustard
  ¼ teaspoon crushed caraway seeds
  4 cups torn assorted greens (such as red oak leaf lettuce, arugula and radicchio)

Heat oil in heavy large skillet over

medium heat. Add mushrooms, leeks, lemon juice and garlic and sauté until tender, about 4 minutes. Add sherry to skillet and bring to boil. Move mushrooms to side of skillet. Add parsley, vinegar, mustard and caraway seeds to skillet and whisk to blend. Toss mushrooms with mustard mixture. Mound assorted greens on plates. Top with mushroom mixture and serve.

MIDDLE EASTERN BREAD SALAD

Try this simple salad as a light lunch or starter. It's a savory accompaniment to roast leg of lamb or grilled fish.

6 SERVINGS

4 pita bread rounds, torn into
   1½- to 2-inch pieces
2 cucumbers, peeled and diced
2 tomatoes, peeled and diced
⅔ cup drained canned chickpeas
   (garbanzo beans)
½ cup fresh lemon juice
½ cup chopped fresh mint leaves
½ cup coarsely chopped fresh
   cilantro
⅓ cup olive oil (preferably
   extra-virgin)
¼ cup Kalamata olives*
6 romaine lettuce leaves, thinly sliced
3 green onions, thinly sliced
3 garlic cloves, finely chopped
1 teaspoon salt
⅔ cup plain yogurt

Preheat oven to 400°F. Place pita bread on baking sheet. Bake until lightly toasted, about 5 minutes. Transfer to large bowl and cool. Add all remaining ingredients except yogurt to bread and toss gently. Divide salad among plates. Top with dollops of yogurt and serve.

Black, brine-cured Kalamata olives are available at Greek and Italian markets and some supermarkets.

PLANTING THE PERFECT SALAD

Raising your own salad is a fun-and-flavor adventure, but it stops being fun if the garden gets to be boss. "Blest be agriculture," said a nineteenth-century sage, "if one does not have too much of it." *Plan* is the first part of *planting*.

If you have a planting space as small as 10 by 12 feet, getting full sun for the greater part of the day, you can grow your own salad. Don't be put off by ponderous dissertations on soil preparation and the mysteries of the pH factor. The ideal planting medium is one-third soil, one-third compost or leaf mold, one-third manure. But if you are just starting out and don't feel that ambitious, do it the simple way: Pick your spot, dig to a depth of 10 or 12 inches, pulverize the soil, rake it smooth, water well, then wait several days for the soil to settle, before planting. You can equalize things a bit when the plants are three or four inches high by giving them a side dressing of manure, or a complete fertilizer—one containing nitrogen, phosphorus and potassium in a 5-10-10 ratio. The numbers will be on the label.

If your planting space is a patio, balcony or window sill, try container gardening—what a way to grow! Containers can be almost any size and shape, but the depth must be adequate to allow for good root development. Whatever you use—elegant ceramic planters, plastic or clay pots, wooden boxes or half-gallon milk cartons—be sure they have drainage holes. Scatter a layer of crocks (broken bits of clay pots) or pebbles at the bottom of the container before adding the planting mixture. Make it easy on yourself; buy the basic planting mixture in ten-pound sacks at the nursery. Pick up some liquid fish fertilizer, too; container gardening requires extra fertilizing to replace nutrients that are washed away.

Does all this sound like "a hard row to hoe"? It really isn't. As a matter of fact, a wise gardener doesn't even use a hoe. Too much danger of damaging surface roots.

PLANTING THE PERFECT SALAD

If you're just getting into gardening, you'll need tools, of course. Don't over-buy; a spade (or spading fork) and a trowel will be sufficient until you find out how deep your gardening enthusiasm goes. Be firm, as you browse in garden center or hardware store; otherwise you may wind up with a garage or storeroom full of unused and expensive implements—a real tool's paradise!

And skip the chemical pesticides. These are plants we're raising to *eat!* For pests that you can't wash off with the hose or pick off with those absolutely wonderful tools called fingers, use derris, rotenone or pyrethrum. These are botanicals (pesticides that are derived from plants) and are nontoxic to people and animals.

You may prefer to start with young plants (seedlings), available at the nursery or garden center, although it's a little like coming into a play in the middle of the first act. When you start from seeds, planting directions are right there on the packet—a very special advantage. But either way, with the constant improvements in the horticultural field, gardening is an adventure. Such developments as "burpless" cucumbers or easy-to-peel tomatoes may not be another giant step for mankind, but they add to the fun and rewards of growing your own salad.

And once you taste the difference between your homegrown produce and the tasteless vegetables from the supermarket bins, you probably will want to grow your own salad through as much of the year as your climate allows.

Get ready—get set—GROW!

Main Courses

Scan the following pages and you'll instantly see how dramatically our attitudes towards food have changed. Sure, hearty fare still holds its appeal; but even robust red meat dishes like Swiss Steak enjoy fresher, cleaner tastes thanks to lighter cooking techniques. And an abundance of poultry and seafood dishes—from Lowfat Turkey Stroganoff to Orange- and Basil-Marinated Swordfish—attests to the healthier turn our tastebuds have taken.

Beef

GRILLED PEPPERED STEAKS

Offer with steamed green beans as part of supper Friday night. A rich Cabernet Sauvignon is a perfect accompaniment.

8 SERVINGS

¾ cup olive oil
⅓ cup red wine vinegar
4½ tablespoons Dijon mustard
4 large garlic cloves, minced
2 large shallots or green onions, chopped
1 tablespoon plus 1 teaspoon coarsely ground black pepper
1 tablespoon minced fresh thyme or 1 teaspoon dried, crumbled
1 tablespoon minced fresh rosemary or 1 teaspoon dried, crumbled
1 teaspoon salt
3 flank steaks (about 1¼ pound each)
Pepper

Fresh thyme sprigs (garnish)
Fresh rosemary sprigs (garnish)

Whisk first 9 ingredients in medium bowl to blend. Place steaks in single layer in large baking dish. Pour marinade over and turn steaks to coat. Cover and refrigerate overnight.

Prepare barbecue (medium-high heat). Remove steaks from marinade and season all sides generously with pepper. Grill steaks to desired doneness, about 4 minutes per side for medium-rare. Thinly slice steaks diagonally across grain. Arrange slices on platter. Garnish with thyme and rosemary and serve.

BEEF BRISKET BRAISED WITH DRIED FRUIT, YAMS AND CARROTS

This can be prepared one day ahead. Serve steamed broccoli on the side.

8 SERVINGS

3 tablespoons vegetable oil
3 medium onions, chopped

4 large garlic cloves, chopped
1 teaspoon paprika
½ teaspoon ground allspice
¼ teaspoon dried crushed red pepper
3½ cups chicken stock or canned broth
1½ cups dry red wine
3 bay leaves

1 4-pound boneless first-cut beef brisket
Paprika
1 6-ounce package dried apricots
1½ cups pitted prunes

3 pounds yams, peeled, cut into 1½-inch pieces
6 large carrots, peeled, cut into 1½-inch pieces
Minced fresh parsley (garnish)

Preheat oven to 325°F. Heat oil in heavy large pot or Dutch oven over medium-high heat. Add onions and garlic and cook until beginning to brown, stirring frequently, about 15 minutes. Add 1 teaspoon paprika, allspice and crushed red pepper and stir 20 seconds. Add chicken stock, wine and bay leaves. Boil 10 minutes to blend flavors.

Sprinkle brisket with paprika and rub in. Add brisket to pot, fat side up. Add dried apricots and pitted prunes. Cover and bake 1½ hours.

Add yams and carrots to pot. Cover and cook until brisket is very tender, about 2½ hours longer. Remove from oven and let stand 20 minutes. Remove brisket from pot and slice thinly across grain. Arrange on platter. Degrease pan juices. Spoon pan juices over meat. Arrange fruit and vegetables around meat. Garnish with minced fresh parsley and serve. (*Can be prepared 2 days ahead. Cover and refrigerate before slicing meat. To serve, remove meat from pot and slice thinly across grain. Remove any solid fat from sauce. Return sliced meat to pot. Place pot in 325°F oven and bake until brisket is heated through, about 30 minutes.*)

CONTEMPORARY SWISS STEAK

Serve with green beans and mashed potatoes, followed by freshly baked, peak-of-the-season pears and whipped cream.

4 SERVINGS

3 tablespoons all purpose flour
¼ teaspoon salt
¼ teaspoon pepper
1 pound cubed steak, cut into 4 pieces

4 tablespoons vegetable oil

1 large onion, thinly sliced
1 large celery stalk, sliced
1 medium carrot, very thinly sliced
1 large garlic clove, minced
1 14½-ounce can stewed tomatoes
½ cup dry red wine
1 teaspoon dried oregano, crumbled
1 teaspoon dried savory, crumbled
Salt and pepper
2 tablespoons chopped fresh parsley (garnish)

Combine flour, salt and pepper in shallow dish. Dredge both sides of steak pieces lightly in flour mixture. Reserve remaining flour.

Heat 2 tablespoons oil in heavy large skillet over high heat. In 2 batches, cook steak pieces until brown, about 2 minutes per side. Transfer to plate.

Add remaining 2 tablespoons oil to skillet. Reduce heat to medium. Add onion, celery and carrot. Cover skillet and cook until vegetables are tender, stirring occasionally, about 8 minutes. Add garlic and reserved flour and cook 1 minute, stirring occasionally. Add stewed tomatoes with their liquid, wine, oregano and savory. Return steaks and any accumulated juices to skillet, spooning vegetables over. Bring to simmer. Reduce heat to low. Cover skillet and cook steaks until tender, about 10 minutes. Uncover skillet and simmer 2 minutes to thicken gravy. Season with salt and pepper. Transfer to platter. Garnish with parsley and serve.

Veal

GRILLED VEAL CHOPS WITH ONION AND RED PEPPER CHUTNEY

Offer a Pinot Noir to go with the meal.

4 SERVINGS

⅓ cup fresh lemon juice
¼ cup olive oil
2 tablespoons chopped fresh thyme
2 tablespoons minced shallot
1 garlic clove, minced
4 1-inch-thick veal chops (about 10 ounces each)
Salt and pepper

Onion and Red Pepper Chutney (see recipe)

Mix first 5 ingredients in small bowl. Place veal in shallow dish. Pour marinade over. Turn to coat. Let stand 1 hour at room temperature.

Prepare barbecue (medium-high heat). Remove veal from marinade. Season veal with salt and pepper. Grill to desired doneness, about 5 minutes per side for medium-rare. Transfer to plates. Top with chutney and serve.

ONION AND RED PEPPER CHUTNEY

This pungent chutney is also nice with pork or chicken.

MAKES ABOUT 1⅓ CUPS

4 red bell peppers

1 tablespoon olive oil
1 red onion, halved, thinly sliced
1 jalapeño chili, halved
2 garlic cloves, chopped
½ cinnamon stick
1 bay leaf
2 tablespoons red wine vinegar
¼ cup chicken stock or canned broth
1 teaspoon tomato paste

Char peppers over gas flame or in broiler until blackened on all sides. Wrap in paper bag and let stand 10 minutes to steam. Peel, seed and coarsely chop roasted peppers.

Heat oil in heavy large skillet over medium-high heat. Add onion and cook until deep golden brown, stirring frequently, about 10 minutes. Add bell peppers, jalapeño, garlic, cinnamon and bay leaf and sauté 2 minutes. Add vinegar, then stock and tomato paste. Reduce heat and simmer until chutney is thick and chunky, stirring occasionally, about 20 minutes. Discard jalapeño, cinnamon and bay leaf. Cool. (*Can be prepared 3 days ahead. Cover and chill. Bring to room temperature before serving.*)

GRILLED VEAL CHOPS WITH DOUBLE-TOMATO RELISH

Sun-dried tomatoes combine with fresh plum tomatoes in this relish. Serve with buttered fettuccine noodles, steamed yellow or green beans, and apricot halves drizzled with Amaretto for dessert.

4 SERVINGS

¼ cup finely chopped drained oil-packed sun-dried tomatoes

½ pound finely chopped plum tomatoes

1 garlic clove, minced

2 tablespoons minced fresh basil or ½ teaspoon dried, crumbled and mixed with 2 tablespoons minced fresh parsley

1½ tablespoons olive oil

1 teaspoon balsamic vinegar or red wine vinegar

¼ to ½ teaspoon hot pepper sauce (such as Tabasco)

4 1-inch-thick loin, rib or T-bone veal chops (about 8 ounces each)

Salt and pepper

2 tablespoons olive oil

In medium bowl, combine sun-dried tomatoes, plum tomatoes, garlic, basil, 1½ tablespoons olive oil, balsamic vinegar and hot sauce. Cover and let stand at room temperature at least 15 minutes. *(Can be prepared 4 hours ahead and refrigerated.)*

Prepare barbecue (high heat). Season both sides of veal chops lightly with salt and pepper. Brush both sides with olive oil. Cook chops to desired doneness, about 5 minutes per side for medium-rare. Transfer cooked chops to platter. Spoon ¼ of tomato relish atop each chop and serve.

Lamb

LEG OF LAMB WITH MINT PESTO

20 SERVINGS

LAMB

2 6-pound legs of lamb, boned, butterflied

Salt and pepper

8 tablespoons vegetable oil

PESTO

2¼ cups packed fresh mint leaves

1 cup packed fresh parsley leaves

½ cup walnuts

2 garlic cloves

1½ cups olive oil

6 tablespoons fresh lime juice

5 teaspoons sugar

1½ teaspoons salt

FOR LAMB: Preheat oven to 350°F. Cut ¼- to ½-inch slits in thick portions of legs of lamb. Cover with plastic wrap.

Pound to uniform thickness. Pat lamb dry with paper towels. Cut each leg of lamb in half crosswise. Season lamb generously with salt and pepper. Heat 2 tablespoons vegetable oil in heavy large skillet over medium-high heat until very hot. Add 1 lamb piece and cook until brown on 1 side, about 2 minutes. Arrange lamb browned side up in heavy large roasting pan. Brown remaining lamb pieces in remaining vegetable oil in 3 more batches. Divide lamb between 2 large roasting pans. Transfer lamb to oven and roast to desired doneness, about 15 minutes for medium-rare. Remove lamb from pans and cool completely. Cover and refrigerate lamb until well chilled. (*Lamb can be prepared to this point 1 day ahead.*)

FOR PESTO: Combine fresh mint leaves, fresh parsley leaves, walnuts and garlic cloves in processor and blend to paste. Gradually add olive oil through feed tube and blend until smooth. Blend in fresh lime juice, sugar and salt. (*Can be prepared 1 day ahead. Pour ½-inch layer of olive oil over pesto. Cover and refrigerate. Bring pesto to room temperature before serving.*)

Cut lamb into ¼-inch-thick slices. Arrange on platter and serve with pesto.

SPICED LAMB AND VEGETABLE KEBABS

Meat left even briefly in this India-inspired yogurt marinade will be tenderized slightly and laced with exotic flavor. Basmati rice pilaf and a big green salad are suitable accompaniments. Offer fresh cherries and purchased or homemade sugar cookies for dessert.

4 SERVINGS

1 cup plain lowfat yogurt
1 tablespoon fresh lime juice
2 teaspoons minced fresh ginger
1½ teaspoons ground cumin
1 garlic clove, minced
¼ teaspoon cayenne pepper
1¼ to 1½ pounds leg of lamb, cut into 16 large cubes

3 yellow summer squash, cut into 12 ½-inch-thick pieces
1 red bell pepper, cut into 12 squares
½ red onion, cut into 12 ½-inch-thick pieces
2 tablespoons vegetable oil

Combine yogurt, lime juice, ginger, cumin, garlic and cayenne in large bowl. Add lamb; stir to coat lamb evenly with yogurt mixture. Marinate at least 20 minutes. (*Can be prepared 1 day ahead. Cover and refrigerate.*)

Prepare barbecue grill (high heat). Alternate 4 lamb cubes, 3 squash pieces, 3 red pepper squares and 3 onion pieces on each of four 12-inch-long skewers. Brush meat and vegetables with oil. Grill until meat is cooked to desired doneness, turning and brushing with oil occasionally, about 10 minutes for medium-rare. Transfer skewers to platter and serve.

Savory Mint Lamb Chops

A rub of exotic spices, fresh mint, garlic and oil creates a crust that seals in juices as the lamb broils. Steamed couscous and sautéed zucchini strips make ideal accompaniments. A refreshing dessert? Try lime sherbet sprinkled with toasted coconut.

4 SERVINGS

¼ cup olive oil
¼ cup chopped fresh mint
4 large garlic cloves, minced
2 teaspoons salt
2 teaspoons ground cumin
1 teaspoon ground coriander
1 teaspoon cayenne pepper
1 teaspoon pepper
8 1- to 1½-inch-thick lamb loin
   chops (about 5 ounces each),
   trimmed

   Fresh mint sprigs (garnish)

Mix olive oil, chopped fresh mint, minced garlic, salt, cumin, coriander and both peppers in small bowl. Spread herb mixture over both sides of lamb chops. Transfer lamb chops to broiler pan. Let stand 10 minutes.

Preheat broiler. Broil chops until brown and crusty but still medium-rare inside, about 4 minutes per side. Arrange chops on platter, garnish with fresh mint sprigs and serve.

Poultry

Turkey Meat Loaf with Sun-dried Tomatoes

A healthful new take on an old favorite.

4 SERVINGS

1 pound ground turkey
1 onion, chopped
1 cup fresh breadcrumbs
1 egg, beaten to blend
½ cup toasted pine nuts
12 sun-dried tomatoes in oil,
   drained, chopped
⅓ cup milk
2 teaspoons chopped fresh rosemary
   or ½ teaspoon dried, crumbled
2 teaspoons chopped fresh oregano
   or ½ teaspoon dried, crumbled
   Salt and pepper

Preheat oven to 375°F. Combine first 9 ingredients in large bowl. Season with salt and pepper and mix well. Transfer mixture to 8½x4½-inch loaf pan. Bake until loaf pulls away from sides of pan and top is golden brown, about 50 minutes.

Lowfat Turkey Stroganoff

A mixture of cottage cheese, lowfat yogurt and lemon juice replaces the sour cream in the traditional version of this dish. Ground turkey makes an especially good choice for those watching their cholesterol intake.

4 SERVINGS

2 tablespoons olive oil
1 pound ground turkey

1 medium onion, chopped
2 cups sliced mushrooms
⅓ cup dry white wine
   Dash of nutmeg
   Salt and pepper

1 cup lowfat cottage cheese
½ cup plain lowfat yogurt
1 tablespoon lemon juice
8 ounces fettuccine, freshly cooked
   Paprika

Heat oil in heavy large skillet over medium heat. Add turkey and onion and cook until turkey is brown, stirring occasionally, about 12 minutes. Mix in mushrooms, wine and nutmeg. Season turkey with salt and pepper. Reduce heat. Simmer 15 minutes.

Purée cottage cheese, yogurt and lemon juice in blender or processor until smooth. Add to turkey and stir until heated through (do not boil). Place fettuccine on platter. Pour turkey over. Sprinkle with paprika and serve.

TURKEY TONNATO

Here, turkey stands in for the traditional veal in a do-ahead entrée. Have your butcher bone, roll and tie the turkey breast.

8 SERVINGS

TURKEY

1 3½-pound boned, rolled and tied turkey breast
3 anchovies, cut into ½-inch pieces
1 large garlic clove, slivered
2 14½-ounce cans chicken broth
2 cups dry white wine
2 onions, quartered
2 carrots, cut into 2-inch pieces
4 fresh parsley sprigs
2 bay leaves

SAUCE

1 6½-ounce can white-meat tuna packed in water, well drained
5 anchovies
3 tablespoons fresh lemon juice
3 tablespoons drained capers
1¼ cup extra-virgin olive oil

1 8-ounce jar mayonnaise (1 cup plus 1 tablespoon)

   Chopped fresh Italian parsley
   Drained capers
2 lemons, halved lengthwise, sliced

FOR TURKEY: Make slits in turkey with tip of small sharp knife; put 1 anchovy piece and 1 garlic silver into each slit. Place turkey in large saucepan or Dutch oven. Add all remaining ingredients. Add water to cover. Bring to boil. Reduce heat, cover partially and simmer until meat thermometer inserted in center of turkey registers 140°F, about 1 hour. Turn off heat and let turkey cool in cooking liquid.

FOR SAUCE: Purée tuna, anchovies, lemon juice and 3 tablespoons capers in processor until very smooth, scraping down sides of work bowl occasionally. With machine running, gradually mix in oil and blend until creamy. Add mayonnaise and just blend using on/off turns (do not overmix).

Remove turkey from broth (reserve broth for another use). Cut off string and pull off turkey skin. Slice turkey into thin rounds. Coat platter with some of sauce. Top with single layer of turkey slices. Spread turkey with more sauce. Sprinkle generously with parsley and capers. Continue layering turkey, sauce, parsley and capers until all of turkey is used. Surround with lemon slices. Cover with plastic; chill turkey and any remaining sauce separately for at least 8 hours. (*Can be prepared 2 days ahead.*) Let turkey stand at room temperature 1 hour. Serve, passing any remaining sauce separately.

STUFFED GAME HENS WITH RASPBERRY SAUCE

An elegant main course that's ready in 40 minutes.

4 SERVINGS

¼ teaspoon pepper
¼ teaspoon garlic powder

2 1½-pound Cornish game hens
2 cups cooked packaged long-grain and wild rice mix (half of uncooked 6.25-ounce package)
¼ cup plus 2 teaspoons butter
¼ cup honey

1 10-ounce package frozen whole unsweetened raspberries, thawed
¼ cup water
2 tablespoons sugar
1 tablespoon grated lemon peel

Preheat oven to 450°F. Combine pepper and garlic powder in bowl. Pat hens dry inside and out. Season cavities with half of pepper mixture. Fill cavities with rice. Close cavities using skewers. Tuck wing tips under. Place hens in roasting pan. Melt butter with honey in small saucepan. Brush over hens. Sprinkle with remaining pepper mixture. Bake hens until juices run clear when thighs are pierced in thickest part, turning and basting frequently with honey-butter mixture, 35 to 40 minutes.

Meanwhile, combine remaining 4 ingredients in heavy medium saucepan over medium-high heat. Cook until thick, stirring frequently, about 10 minutes. Sieve to remove seeds if desired.

Transfer hens to cutting board. Cut each in half. Transfer hens with stuffing to plates. Spoon sauce over.

TURKEY CUTLETS WITH ALMONDS AND SNOW PEAS

This recipe is about as far from Thanksgiving dinner as June is from November. Round out the main course with dinner rolls and saffron rice. Indulge yourself afterward with rich chocolate ice cream sprinkled with raspberries.

4 SERVINGS

1 pound turkey breast cutlets (about ¼ to ⅓ inch thick)
Salt and pepper
4 tablespoons (½ stick) butter

⅓ cup sliced almonds (about 1 ounce)
3 garlic cloves, minced

12 ounces snow peas, trimmed,
  halved diagonally
1 tablespoon minced fresh tarragon
  or ½ teaspoon dried, crumbled
½ cup dry white wine

Pat turkey dry with paper towels. Season with salt and pepper. Melt 2 tablespoons butter in heavy large skillet over high heat. Add turkey to skillet and fry until light golden and just cooked through, about 1 minute per side. Transfer turkey to platter. Tent with foil to keep warm.

Reduce heat to medium. Melt 1 tablespoon more butter in same skillet. Add almonds and sauté until golden, stirring constantly, about 30 seconds. Using slotted spoon, transfer almonds to small dish. Melt remaining 1 tablespoon butter in same skillet. Add garlic and stir to coat with butter. Add snow peas and tarragon and sauté until snow peas are just tender, about 2 minutes. Arrange snow pea mixture over turkey. Pour wine into skillet and boil until liquid is slightly reduced, scraping up any browned bits, about 3 minutes. Season sauce to taste with salt and pepper. Spoon sauce over turkey and snow peas. Sprinkle almonds over and serve.

CARIBBEAN CHICKEN AND VEGETABLE KEBABS

Offer your favorite corn bread along with the kebabs and salads.

12 SERVINGS

8 large garlic cloves, minced
2 teaspoons ground coriander
2 teaspoons ground turmeric
2 teaspoons dried mustard
2 teaspoons ground cloves
2 teaspoons chili powder
1 teaspoon aniseed
2 pounds boneless skinless chicken
  breasts, cut into 1-inch pieces
1⅓ pounds boneless skinless chicken
  thighs, cut into 1-inch pieces
4 red onions, cut into 1-inch pieces
6 yellow summer squash, cut into
  ½-inch-thick rounds
4 chayote squash, halved lengthwise,
  cut into ¼-inch-thick slices or
  4 zucchini, cut into ½-inch-thick
  rounds
1½ cups olive oil
⅓ cup fresh lime juice

12 (about) bamboo skewers
  Salt and pepper

Combine garlic, coriander, turmeric, dried mustard, ground cloves, chili powder and aniseed in small bowl. Place chicken in one glass baking dish and vegetables in another. Sprinkle each with half of spice mixture. Add half of olive oil and half of fresh lime juice to each and mix to coat well. Cover and refrigerate 6 to 8 hours.

Soak skewers in water 30 minutes. Drain. Alternate chicken and vegetables on skewers. (*Can be prepared 2 hours ahead. Cover and refrigerate.*)

Prepare barbecue (medium heat)

or preheat broiler. Season kebabs with salt and pepper. Grill until chicken is cooked through, about 5 minutes per side. Transfer to platter.

LIGHT CHICKEN AND CHEESE ENCHILADAS

Instead of frying the tortillas here, soften them in a hot, dry skillet. That makes them pliable without adding calories.

6 SERVINGS

2 large chicken breast halves
   (about 1½ pounds total)
2 cups chicken stock or canned
   low-salt broth
1 cup water
1 garlic clove, minced
1 bay leaf
2 green onions, thinly sliced
¼ cup chopped fresh cilantro
½ teaspoon dried oregano, crumbled
½ teaspoon salt
¼ teaspoon pepper

2 tablespoons vegetable oil

3 garlic cloves, minced
2 tablespoons chili powder
3 tablespoons all purpose flour
1 tablespoon ground cumin
⅛ teaspoon ground cinnamon
⅓ cup canned tomato sauce

12 6-inch-diameter corn tortillas
¾ cup grated sharp cheddar cheese
   (about 3 ounces)

Arrange chicken breast halves in heavy medium saucepan. Add stock, water, garlic and bay leaf. Bring to boil. Reduce heat, cover and simmer until chicken is cooked through, about 12 minutes. Transfer chicken to bowl using slotted spoon and cool. Discard bay leaf. Reserve poaching liquid. Peel skin off chicken and remove meat from bones. Tear meat into strips. Place in large bowl. Mix in green onions, cilantro, oregano, salt and pepper.

Heat 2 tablespoons oil in heavy medium saucepan over medium-high heat. Add 3 minced garlic cloves and sauté 30 seconds. Add chili powder and sauté 1 minute. Add flour, cumin and cinnamon and stir 1 minute (mixture will be dry). Whisk in 1 cup reserved poaching liquid. Add remaining poaching liquid and tomato sauce. Cook until thick and smooth, whisking frequently, 5 minutes. Cool slightly.

Lightly oil 13x9x2-inch baking dish. Heat heavy medium skillet over high heat until hot. Add 1 tortilla and cook until heated through, turning frequently. Using tongs as aid, grasp tortilla and dip into sauce, coating both sides. Place in prepared dish. Spoon 3 tablespoons chicken filling in strip near bottom edge of tortilla. Starting at filled end, roll tortilla up jellyroll style. Turn seam side down. Repeat with remaining tortillas, sauce and filling. Spoon any remaining sauce over enchiladas. Sprinkle with cheese. Cover with foil. (*Can be made 1 day ahead; chill.*)

Position rack in top third of oven and preheat to 425°F. Bake enchiladas

10 minutes. Uncover and bake until hot and bubbling, about 10 minutes.

SOY-LEMON CHICKEN

6 SERVINGS

6 chicken breast halves
½ cup soy sauce
½ cup fresh lemon juice
1 tablespoon Oriental sesame oil

Toasted sesame seeds
Thinly sliced green onions

Place chicken skin side up in 9x13-inch baking dish. Pour soy sauce and lemon juice over chicken. Drizzle chicken with Oriental sesame oil. Marinate chicken in refrigerator 1 to 2 hours.

Preheat oven to 350°F. Cover chicken and bake 35 minutes. Uncover and continue baking until chicken is cooked through, about 15 minutes longer. Transfer to platter; garnish with sesame seeds and green onions.

ROASTED MUSTARD-CHIVE GAME HENS

For a fast and delicious meal, bake rice pilaf in the oven alongside the halved game hens. Round out the menu with steamed whole green beans and, for a sweet finish, a rhubarb pie or cobbler.

4 SERVINGS

12 tablespoons (1½ sticks) unsalted butter, room temperature
½ cup minced fresh chives
2 tablespoons plus 2 teaspoons Dijon mustard
4 1- to 1½-pound Cornish game hens, halved lengthwise
Salt and pepper

2 cups dry white wine
Whole fresh chives (garnish)

Position rack in center of oven and preheat oven to 450°F.

Mix 12 tablespoons butter, ½ cup minced chives and Dijon mustard in medium bowl. Use fingertips to loosen skin from breast portion of game hen halves. Spread 1 tablespoon chive butter over entire breast portion under loosened skin of each game hen half. Chill remaining chive butter. Season game hens lightly with salt and pepper. Place game hens, skin side up, in large baking pan. Roast until game hens are golden brown and juices run clear when thighs are pierced, about 30 minutes.

Transfer hens to platter. Tent loosely with foil to keep warm. Place baking pan over medium-high heat. Add wine to pan drippings and boil until sauce is reduced to ¾ cup, scraping up browned bits, about 10 minutes. Gradually whisk in remaining chive butter. Spoon sauce over hens, garnish with whole fresh chives and serve.

ROAST CHICKEN WITH OLIVES AND POTATOES

A superb dish—and what could be simpler? Large roasting chickens can be ordered from the supermarket or butcher if you call a day or two ahead. Serve steamed green beans and crusty French bread on the side and pour a Côtes du Rhône or Tavel rosé.

4 SERVINGS

1 7-pound roasting chicken
6 tablespoons olive paste (olivada)*
2 bay leaves
  Olive oil
  Salt and pepper
4 tablespoons fresh thyme leaves

4 medium russet potatoes, peeled, cut into 1½-inch pieces
2 tablespoons olive oil
½ cup Kalamata** olives

  Fresh thyme leaves

Preheat oven to 450°F. Slide hand between chicken skin and meat over breast and legs to form pockets. Spread 4 table-spoons olive paste over breast and leg meat of chicken. Spread remaining 2 tablespoons olive paste in cavity of chicken. Place bay leaves in cavity. Tie legs together to hold shape. Rub olive oil into chicken skin. Sprinkle with salt and pepper. Sprinkle with 2 tablespoons thyme. Place chicken in large roasting pan.

Place potatoes in large bowl. Add 2 tablespoons olive oil and salt and pepper to taste and toss to coat. Sprinkle with 2 tablespoons thyme. Add potatoes to pan with chicken. Roast 15 minutes. Reduce oven temperature to 375°F and roast 1 hour longer. Add olives to pan. Continue roasting until juices run clear when chicken is pierced in thickest part of thigh, basting occasionally with pan juices, about 10 minutes.

Transfer chicken to platter. Surround with potatoes and olives. Sprinkle with additional thyme. Pour chicken pan juices into large cup and degrease. Serve chicken, passing pan juices separately.

*Olive paste, also called olivada, is available at Italian markets and specialty foods stores. If unavailable, purée ½ cup pitted black, brine-cured olives (such as Kalamata) in processor or blender.

**Kalamata olives are available at Greek and Italian markets and at some specialty foods stores.

ROAST CHICKEN WITH TURNIPS, CARROTS AND WILD MUSHROOMS

6 SERVINGS

2 3- to 3¼-pound chickens
4 tablespoons olive oil
8 garlic cloves, flattened
4 tablespoons minced fresh thyme or 4 teaspoons dried, crumbled
2 tablespoons chopped fresh rosemary or 2 teaspoons dried, crumbled
1 teaspoon salt
1 teaspoon pepper
6 medium turnips, peeled, quartered

6 carrots, peeled, halved lengthwise, cut into 3-inch-long pieces

1 tablespoon unsalted butter
¾ pound wild mushrooms (such as shiitake or chanterelle) or button mushrooms
Salt and pepper

Preheat oven to 350°F. Rub each chicken with 1 tablespoon oil. Rub garlic over chickens, then place garlic in chicken cavities. Mix 2 tablespoons thyme with rosemary, ½ teaspoon salt and ½ teaspoon pepper. Rub herb mixture over chickens. Place chickens in large roasting pan. Surround with turnips and carrots. Drizzle remaining 2 tablespoons oil over vegetables. Sprinkle vegetables with remaining 2 tablespoons thyme, ½ teaspoon salt and ½ teaspoon pepper. Roast chickens until juices run clear when thickest part of thighs are pierced, about 1 hour 10 minutes, turning vegetables occasionally. Transfer chickens to platter and tent with foil. Increase heat to 400°F.

Continue roasting vegetables until tender, about 15 minutes.

Meanwhile, melt 1 tablespoon butter in heavy large skillet over high heat. Add mushrooms and sauté until tender, about 10 minutes. Season to taste with salt and pepper.

Spoon vegetables and mushrooms around chickens and serve.

SAUTÉED CHICKEN WITH GARLIC AND ROSEMARY

The piquant garlic and rosemary sauce beautifully complements the richness of the sautéed chicken. If you're not a garlic lover, you'll want to reduce the amount here to suit your taste. Partner the main course with steamed baby carrots and rice with peas; chocolate mousse for dessert would complete this menu nicely.

4 SERVINGS

2 pounds chicken thighs
Salt and pepper

2 tablespoons olive oil
3 large garlic cloves, minced
2 teaspoons chopped fresh rosemary or 1 teaspoon dried, crumbled
1 cup canned chicken broth
2 tablespoons red wine vinegar

Fresh rosemary sprigs (optional garnish)

Season chicken thighs with salt and pepper. Heat oil in heavy large skillet over high heat. Add chicken to skillet and sauté until brown, about 5 minutes per side. Reduce heat to medium-low, cover skillet and fry until chicken is cooked through, about 15 minutes. Transfer chicken to bowl. Discard all but 2 tablespoons drippings from skillet. Add garlic and rosemary to skillet. Cook until just fragrant, stirring constantly, about 1 minute. Add broth and vinegar to skillet. Increase heat and boil until sauce is reduced to ½ cup, scraping up browned bits, about 7 minutes. Season sauce to taste with salt and pepper. Return chicken and any accumulated juices to skillet. Cover and cook over very low heat until chicken is heated, about 10 minutes. Spoon sauce over. Garnish with rosemary if desired.

Fish

ORANGE- AND BASIL-MARINATED SWORDFISH (COVER RECIPE)

The flavorful marinade is also good to use on salmon or halibut. Finish the meal with fresh fruit topped with nonfat yogurt.

4 SERVINGS

⅓ cup packed, thinly sliced fresh basil leaves (about 1 bunch)
¼ cup orange juice
2 tablespoons fresh lemon juice
2 tablespoons olive oil
2 teaspoons grated orange peel

2 12-ounce ¾-inch-thick swordfish steaks
Salt and pepper

4 ⅓-inch-thick orange slices (garnish)
Olive oil
Fresh basil sprigs (garnish)

Combine first 5 ingredients in large baking dish. Add fish to dish, turning to coat with marinade. Marinate 30 minutes to 1 hour in refrigerator.

Prepare barbecue (medium-high heat). Season fish generously with salt and pepper. Grill until cooked through, about 4 minutes per side.

Meanwhile, brush orange slices with olive oil and grill until almost brown, about 2 minutes per side. Transfer swordfish steaks to platter. Garnish with grilled orange slices and basil sprigs and serve.

SHRIMP AND SCALLOP SAUTÉ

New England has a large Portuguese population. Their numbers are most concentrated in Massachusetts fishing centers, such as New Bedford, Gloucester and Provincetown, where they've had an important influence on the cuisine. One of their specialties is fried scallops, Portuguese-style—a sauté of bay scallops in butter with garlic and parsley. This elaboration on the basic dish adds shrimp, mushrooms, green onions and a white wine sauce. Serve it over rice, and offer buttered peas or broccoli on the side.

6 SERVINGS

3 tablespoons butter
3 tablespoons olive oil
6 large garlic cloves, minced
1 pound mushrooms, sliced
2 tablespoons tomato paste
¼ cup dry white wine
¼ cup fresh lemon juice
1 pound medium shrimp, peeled, deveined
1 bunch green onions, sliced

1 pound bay scallops
  Salt and pepper
⅓ cup chopped fresh parsley

Melt butter with olive oil in heavy large skillet over medium heat. Add minced garlic cloves and sauté 1 minute. Increase heat to high, add sliced mushrooms and sauté until just beginning to soften, about 5 minutes. Add tomato paste and stir 30 seconds. Add dry white wine and fresh lemon juice and bring to boil. Add shrimp and sliced green onions and stir 1 minute. Add scallops and stir until shrimp and scallops are cooked through, about 3 minutes. Season to taste with salt and pepper. Sprinkle with chopped fresh parsley and serve immediately.

Sautéed Scallops with Shiitake Mushrooms and Broccoli

2 SERVINGS; CAN BE DOUBLED

1 ounce dried shiitake mushrooms

1 pound broccoli, trimmed, cut
  into florets
¼ cup butter
¾ pound sea scallops, halved
  crosswise
1 bunch green onions, sliced
½ lemon
  Salt and pepper
2 tablespoons toasted pine nuts
  Freshly cooked rice

Place mushrooms in small bowl. Add boiling water to cover. Let stand until softened, about 20 minutes. Drain, reserving 3 tablespoons soaking liquid. Squeeze out any liquid from mushrooms. Cut out stems; cut mushrooms into quarters. Blanch broccoli in large pot of boiling salted water until just crisp-tender. Drain. Refresh with cold water and drain well.

Melt butter in heavy large skillet over medium-high heat. Add mushrooms and sauté 1 minute. Add scallops and green onions and stir until scallops are almost

cooked through. Add broccoli and stir until broccoli is heated through and scallops are opaque. Add reserved shiitake soaking liquid. Squeeze juice of lemon half into skillet. Season mixture with salt and pepper. Sprinkle with nuts. Serve with rice.

Shrimp and Mushrooms in Spicy Black Bean Oyster Sauce

4 SERVINGS

12 medium-sized dried Chinese
   black mushrooms* or dried
   shiitake mushrooms (about
   1 ounce)
1½ cups hot water
 1 pound large uncooked shrimp,
   peeled, deveined
 1 tablespoon dry sherry or dry
   white wine
 2 tablespoons cornstarch

 2 tablespoons oyster sauce*
1½ teaspoons sugar

2 tablespoons salted black beans*
1½ tablespoons minced garlic
1½ tablespoons minced peeled fresh
  ginger
1 tablespoon minced seeded red
  or green chili (such as serrano or
  jalapeño)
2 green onions, finely chopped

¼ cup plus 2 tablespoons peanut oil

Freshly cooked rice

Soak mushrooms in 1½ cups hot water in medium bowl until softened, about 20 minutes. Drain mushrooms, reserving 1 cup soaking liquid. Squeeze out excess moisture. Cut off stems and discard. Cut caps in half. Toss mushrooms, shrimp, sherry and 1 tablespoon cornstarch together in medium bowl to coat evenly. Let stand 15 minutes.

Whisk 1 cup reserved mushroom soaking liquid, oyster sauce, remaining 1 tablespoon cornstarch and sugar in small bowl until cornstarch dissolves. Cover black beans with hot water and soak 1 minute. Drain beans and chop finely. Combine beans in small bowl with garlic, ginger, chili and half of green onions.

Heat ¼ cup oil in wok or heavy large skillet over high heat. Add shrimp mixture and stir-fry until shrimp curl and turn pink, about 2 minutes. Pour contents of wok into sieve to drain shrimp.

Line platter with cooked rice. Heat remaining 2 tablespoons peanut oil in same wok over high heat. Stir-fry black bean mixture until fragrant, about 1 minute. Return shrimp mixture to wok. Stir mushroom liquid mixture and add to wok. Cook until sauce thickens and begins to boil, stirring constantly, about 1 minute. Spoon contents of wok over rice on platter. Garnish with remaining green onions and serve.

Available at Oriental markets and some supermarkets.

SAUTÉED SOLE WITH TOMATO-CAPER COMPOTE

The lemony sauce is a delightful foil for sautéed fish of any type. Complete the easy dinner with boiled new potatoes, steamed asparagus spears, and a purchased chocolate cake for dessert.

4 SERVINGS

¾ cup all purpose flour
¾ teaspoon salt
¾ teaspoon pepper
¾ cup milk
1½ pounds sole fillets

6 tablespoons olive oil

¼ cup butter
1¼ pounds ripe plum tomatoes,
  peeled, seeded, diced
6 tablespoons chopped fresh
  parsley
3 tablespoons fresh lemon juice
1½ tablespoons drained capers

Lemon slices (garnish)

Additional capers (garnish)

Combine flour, salt and pepper in shallow dish. Pour milk into another shallow dish. Dip 1 fish fillet into milk to moisten, then into flour mixture, turning to coat completely. Place fillet on large sheet of waxed paper. Repeat procedure with remaining fillets.

Heat 3 tablespoons oil in heavy large skillet over medium-high heat. Add half of fish to skillet and sauté until light brown and cooked through, about 2 minutes per side. Transfer to platter. Heat 3 more tablespoons oil in same skillet. Sauté remaining fish fillets. Transfer fish to platter.

Melt butter in same skillet. Add tomatoes and simmer until tomatoes are soft, pressing and stirring occasionally, about 5 minutes. Mix in chopped parsley, lemon juice and 1½ tablespoons capers. Cook until ingredients are thickened and reduced to sauce consistency, stirring occasionally, about 5 minutes.

Spoon compote over fish fillets.

Garnish platter with lemon slices and additional capers and serve.

PAN-FRIED CATFISH WITH PEPPER AND LEMON

The crunchy cornmeal crust is great on other firm-fleshed white fish fillets, too. Serve red-cabbage coleslaw and french fries alongside. Offer vanilla pudding with strawberries for dessert.

4 SERVINGS

¼ cup plus 2 tablespoons yellow cornmeal
¼ cup plus 2 tablespoons all purpose flour
1 tablespoon grated lemon peel
½ teaspoon cayenne pepper
Salt
⅔ cup buttermilk
4 6-ounce catfish fillets

2 tablespoons (¼ stick) butter
1 tablespoon vegetable oil
1 tablespoon minced fresh parsley
Lemon wedges (garnish)

Combine cornmeal, flour, lemon peel and cayenne in shallow dish. Season with salt. Pour buttermilk into second dish. Dip 1 fish fillet into buttermilk, then into cornmeal mixture, coating completely. Repeat with remaining fish.

Melt butter with oil in heavy large skillet over medium-high heat. Add fish and cook until crust is golden brown and fish is cooked through, turning once, about 4 minutes per side. Transfer fish to platter. Sprinkle with minced parsley. Garnish with lemon wedges.

RED SNAPPER ROASTED WITH FENNEL AND BREADCRUMBS

If one large fish is difficult to find, two smaller ones can be substituted.

6 SERVINGS

2 fresh fennel bulbs, trimmed, chopped
6 large shallots or green onions, chopped
½ cup chopped fresh Italian parsley

2 cups fresh French breadcrumbs
¼ cup olive oil
  Salt and pepper

1 3½- to 4-pound headless red
  snapper
¼ cup dry white wine
  Olive oil

Combine first 3 ingredients in medium bowl. Transfer 1 cup fennel mixture to large bowl. Add breadcrumbs and ¼ cup olive oil to 1 cup fennel mixture in large bowl. Season with salt and pepper. (*Can be prepared 1 day ahead. Cover fennel mixture and breadcrumb mixture separately and refrigerate.*)

Preheat oven to 450°F. Cut slashes 2 inches apart almost to bone in both sides of fish. Spread half of fennel mixture in bottom of gratin dish or roasting pan. Sprinkle with wine. Spread generous amount of oil over inside and outside of fish. Season inside and out with salt and pepper. Set fish atop fennel mixture in dish. Spread remaining fennel mix-

ture inside fish. Spread breadcrumb mixture over top of fish, pressing to adhere.

Bake fish until just opaque in center, about 45 minutes. Serve with fennel.

HOT-AND-SOUR SHRIMP WITH WATERCRESS AND WALNUTS

A light marinade of sherry and ginger flavors the shrimp, which are stir-fried with red bell peppers and green onions. Watercress makes a colorful bed.

4 SERVINGS

1 pound large uncooked shrimp, peeled, deveined, butterflied
4 tablespoons dry sherry
1 tablespoon grated peeled fresh ginger
½ cup chicken stock or canned broth
2 tablespoons soy sauce
2 tablespoons catsup
1 tablespoon cornstarch

1 tablespoon rice vinegar or white wine vinegar
1 tablespoon sugar
1 tablespoon Oriental sesame oil
¼ tablespoon cayenne pepper

6 teaspoons peanut oil
2 tablespoons chopped walnuts
3 bunches watercress, trimmed
2 medium red bell peppers, cut into 1-inch squares
2 garlic cloves, minced
8 green onions, cut diagonally into 1-inch-long pieces

Combine shrimp, 2 tablespoons sherry and grated ginger in large bowl. Cover and refrigerate for 30 minutes. Mix remaining 2 tablespoons sherry, chicken stock, soy sauce, catsup, cornstarch, rice vinegar, sugar, sesame oil and cayenne pepper in small bowl.

Heat 2 teaspoons peanut oil in wok or heavy large skillet over high heat. Add walnuts and stir-fry 1 minute. Transfer walnuts to plate using slotted spoon. Add watercress to wok and stir-fry until just wilted, about 1 minute. Divide watercress among plates. Add 2 teaspoons peanut oil, bell peppers and garlic to wok and stir-fry 1 minute. Add remaining 2 teaspoons peanut oil, shrimp mixture and onions and stir-fry 1 minute. Stir stock mixture, add to wok and cook sauce until clear and thick, stirring frequently, 2 minutes.

Spoon sauce and shrimp over watercress. Sprinkle with walnuts and serve.

GRILLED TUNA WITH OLIVE-ROSEMARY BUTTER

A simple, sunny dish with the flavors of the south of France. The seasoned butter is our bonus, since the fish is already delicious after its quick marinating in a rosemary vinaigrette. Add a sliced tomato salad and buttered orzo (rice-shaped pasta) for a satisfying meal.

4 SERVINGS

¼ cup (½ stick) unsalted butter, room temperature

1 tablespoon chopped pitted brine-cured olives (such as Kalamata*)
1 tablespoon plus ¼ teaspoon fresh lemon juice
2 teaspoons chopped fresh rosemary or ½ teaspoon dried, crumbled
¼ teaspoon Dijon mustard

3 tablespoons olive oil
⅛ teaspoon pepper
4 8-ounce tuna steaks (1 inch thick)

Fresh rosemary sprigs (optional garnish)

Blend butter, olives, ¼ teaspoon lemon juice, 1 teaspoon rosemary and mustard in small bowl. *(Butter can be prepared up to 2 days ahead. Wrap tightly and refrigerate. Let stand at room temperature 45 minutes before continuing.)*

Whisk olive oil with remaining 1 tablespoon fresh lemon juice, remaining 1 teaspoon rosemary and pepper in shallow dish. Arrange tuna steaks in dish, turn to coat both sides. Let stand 15 minutes.

Prepare barbecue (high heat). Grill tuna until just cooked through, about 4 minutes per side. Transfer to platter. Place 1 tablespoon rosemary butter on each steak. Garnish with rosemary sprigs if desired.

*Black, brine-cured Kalamata olives are available at Greek and Italian markets and some supermarkets.

SALMON STEAKS WITH TOMATILLO-APPLE SALSA

Buttered rice and sautéed zucchini are great side dishes for this tangy salmon recipe. Chocolate ice cream drizzled with coffee liqueur makes a perfect dessert.

4 SERVINGS

5 fresh tomatillos,* husked, chopped (about 1 cup)
1 yellow or green bell pepper, seeded, chopped
1 small unpeeled Red Delicious apple, cored, chopped

½ cup chopped red onion
3 tablespoons chopped fresh
  cilantro
2 tablespoons olive oil
1 tablespoon fresh lemon juice
1 large jalapeño chili, seeded,
  minced
½ teaspoon salt

4 8-ounce salmon steaks (about 1
  inch thick)
  Olive oil
  Salt and pepper

Combine first 9 ingredients in medium bowl. (*Can be prepared 3 hours ahead. Cover and let stand at room temperature.*)

  Preheat broiler. Brush both sides of salmon with olive oil. Season with salt and pepper. Broil salmon 3 inches from heat source until just cooked through, about 5 minutes per side.

  Arrange salmon on platter. Stir salsa well. Spoon some salsa over salmon. Pass extra salsa separately.

*A green, tomato-like vegetable with a paper-thin husk. Available at Latin American markets, special foods stores and some supermarkets.

BAKED RED SNAPPER WITH FENNEL-SCENTED TOMATO SAUCE

Buy an apple tart for dessert.

2 SERVINGS;
CAN BE DOUBLED OR TRIPLED

2 tablespoons olive oil
½ large onion, sliced
1 28-ounce can Italian plum
  tomatoes, drained
¼ cup dry white wine
2 2½x1-inch pieces orange peel
  (orange part only)
¼ teaspoon fennel seeds
⅛ teaspoon dried crushed red pepper
  Salt and pepper

2 ¾-inch-thick red snapper or
  other firm white fish fillets

Preheat oven to 400°F. Heat 1 tablespoon oil in heavy medium skillet over medium heat. Add onion and sauté until tender, about 8 minutes. Add tomatoes, wine, orange peel, fennel seeds and crushed red pepper. Boil gently until reduced to chunky sauce, breaking up tomatoes with spoon, about 12 minutes. Season with salt and pepper. (*Can be prepared 1 day ahead. Cover and chill. Rewarm before continuing.*)

  Pour remaining 1 tablespoon oil into small baking dish. Add fish and turn to coat with oil. Sprinkle with salt and pepper. Spoon warm sauce over fish. Bake until just cooked through, about 20 minutes. Serve immediately.

REDUCING FAT IN YOUR DIET

For a well-balanced diet and to keep blood cholesterol levels healthy, the American Heart Association recommends limiting fat intake to no more than 30 percent of total calories.

- Always remove all visible fat from poultry and meat before cooking.

- Because much of the fat in poultry is in the skin, remove the skin before cooking. Wing tips, which are also high in fat, can be removed as well.

- When shopping for ground beef, purchase the leanest grade. In selecting fish, choose the lean, less oily types, such as snapper, sea bass, swordfish, halibut, sole or monkfish.

- Grilling fish, chicken and all meats enables fat to drip away.

- Before roasting or broiling, place meat on rack in pan so that the meat does not remain in drippings.

- Though chicken is low in fat and cholesterol, turkey has even fewer calories than chicken. Use turkey breast cutlets or fillets in recipes calling for veal scallops. Also try using ground turkey in place of beef in your favorite meat loaf, meatball or chili recipes.

- Fish and chicken can be cooked "en papillote." Place on foil or parchment, add fresh herbs, lemon juice and tomatoes, then fold up and bake. The packet helps seal in flavors and juices.

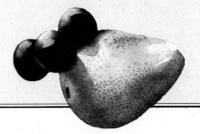

continued on next page

REDUCING FAT IN YOUR DIET

- Poaching chicken or fish in water, stock or white wine results in moist flesh and adds few calories.

- When frying or sautéing, instead of using butter, rub a drop of polyunsaturated vegetable oil or olive oil over the skillet. Or use nonstick cookware, which requires little or no oil.

- Prepare soups and stews one day before serving and refrigerate overnight. When chilled, fat will rise to top and solidify, so it's easy to remove.

- For most puréed vegetable soups, low-salt chicken stock or lowfat milk can be substituted for cream.

- Be careful with nondairy creamers, whipped toppings and sour cream substitutes. Many contain coconut oil, palm oil or palm kernel oil, which are very high in saturated fats.

- When you crave something sweet for dessert, try the 98 percent fat-free ice cream in most supermarkets.

- Lowfat, cholesterol-free cakes and other baked goods are now offered by a growing number of food companies. Sara Lee and Entenmann's, in particular, have delicious and healthful new versions of coffee cakes, pound cakes, streusels and Danishes.

Pastas, Pizzas & Sandwiches

More than any other foods, pastas, pizzas, and sandwiches may well be the sensations of the '90s. High in carbohydrates and low in fat, they cater perfectly to our enlightened eating attitudes. And the international variety of tastes they offer—from Rotelle with Smoked Turkey, Broccoli and Peppers to Hot-and-Sour Thai Noodle Stir-Fry, Mesquite-Grilled Pizza to Sandwich Niçoise—make every meal a fresh experience.

Pasta

ROTELLE WITH SMOKED TURKEY, BROCCOLI AND PEPPERS

A simple and satisfying pasta to savor at the end of a frazzling day. Fresh broccoli cooks in less time than it will take for the frozen variety to thaw (and it tastes better, too), but packaged florets from the freezer can be substituted (following package directions). The turkey's smoky flavor is important to the dish; smoked chicken or baked ham would also make good eating. The recipe doubles easily.

2 SERVINGS

2 cups small broccoli florets
5 ounces rotelle or fusilli pasta

2 tablespoons (¼ stick) unsalted
   butter
2 tablespoons olive oil
2 garlic cloves, minced

¼ teaspoon dried red pepper flakes
8 ounces smoked turkey, skin
   removed, diced

⅓ cup jar-packed roasted red
   peppers, drained, diced
½ cup chicken stock or canned
   broth
Freshly grated Romano cheese

Cook broccoli in large pot of boiling salted water until crisp-tender, about 2 minutes. Using slotted spoon, transfer broccoli to bowl of ice water to cool; reserve water in pot. Drain broccoli and pat dry. Return water to boil. Add pasta and cook until just tender but still firm to bite, stirring occasionally to prevent sticking. Drain thoroughly.

Meanwhile, melt butter with olive oil in heavy large skillet over low heat. Add garlic and red pepper flakes and sauté until garlic is tender, about 3 minutes. Add turkey and sauté until heated through, about 4 minutes.

Mix broccoli, pasta, roasted peppers

and stock into turkey mixture. Increase heat to high and cook until pasta has absorbed most of liquid, stirring frequently, about 4 minutes. Divide pasta between plates and serve, passing Romano cheese separately.

PASTA WITH LEMON-PARSLEY CLAM SAUCE

Crusty bread and a curly endive and radicchio salad make excellent accompaniments for the pasta. For dessert, drizzle hot fudge sauce over coffee ice cream.

4 SERVINGS

3 tablespoons butter
5 tablespoons olive oil
5 large garlic cloves, chopped
2 10-ounce cans whole baby clams,
   drained, juices reserved
½ cup (about) bottled clam juice
⅔ cup dry white wine
1½ teaspoons dried marjoram,
   crumbled

¼ teaspoon dried crushed red pepper
2 tablespoons fresh lemon juice
¾ teaspoon grated lemon peel

12 ounces capellini (angel hair)
    pasta or spaghettini
½ cup chopped fresh parsley
    Salt and pepper
    Thin lemon slices (garnish)

Melt butter with oil in heavy large skillet over medium heat. Add garlic and sauté 1 minute. Measure reserved clam juices. Add enough bottled clam juice to equal 1½ cups. Add 1½ cups clam juice, wine, marjoram and dried pepper to skillet. Boil until reduced to 1¼ cups, about 7 minutes. Add clams, lemon juice and lemon peel. Simmer 2 minutes.

Meanwhile, cook capellini in large pot of boiling salted water until just tender but still firm to bite, stirring occasionally to prevent sticking. Drain well.

Add pasta and all but 1 tablespoon parsley to sauce. Toss to coat pasta. Season with salt and pepper. Divide among 4 plates. Sprinkle with remaining parsley. Garnish with lemon slices.

FETTUCCINE WITH SPINACH-RICOTTA SAUCE

Serve this colorful pasta with crisp breadsticks and thinly sliced red and yellow bell peppers drizzled with olive oil and red wine vinegar. For dessert, offer fresh strawberries.

4 SERVINGS

3 tablespoons olive oil
1 medium onion, chopped
3 large garlic cloves, minced
1 tablespoon all purpose flour
2 cups milk (do not use lowfat or nonfat)
1 10-ounce package frozen chopped spinach, thawed, well drained
1 cup ricotta cheese
⅓ cup freshly grated Parmesan cheese
10 oil-packed sun-dried tomatoes, drained, cut into thin strips
3 tablespoons chopped fresh basil or 2 teaspoons dried, crumbled
¼ teaspoon ground nutmeg
    Salt and pepper

1 pound fettuccine

⅓ cup minced green onions
⅓ cup toasted pine nuts
    Coarsely ground pepper
    Freshly grated Parmesan cheese

Heat oil in heavy medium saucepan over medium heat. Add onion and cook until translucent, stirring occasionally, about 4 minutes. Add garlic and cook 1 minute. Stir in flour and cook 1 minute. Gradually whisk in milk and cook until sauce is smooth and bubbling, stirring constantly, about 4 minutes. Mix in spinach, ricotta, ⅓ cup Parmesan, sun-dried tomatoes, basil and nutmeg. Season to taste with salt and pepper. Simmer over medium-low heat until heated through, stirring occasionally, about 5 minutes.

Meanwhile, cook fettuccine in large pot of rapidly boiling salted water until just tender but still firm to bite. Drain.

Transfer pasta to platter. Spoon sauce over. Garnish with green onions and pine nuts. Sprinkle with coarsely ground pepper. Serve, passing additional Parmesan cheese separately.

HOT-AND-SOUR THAI NOODLE STIR-FRY

In this vegetarian entrée, thin noodles are tossed with tofu, colorful vegetables and a wonderfully spicy Thai-style peanut and lime sauce. Start the meal off by serving vegetable broth with chopped green onion tops. For dessert, try coconut ice cream or a fruit sorbet.

4 SERVINGS

3 garlic cloves
⅔ cup creamy peanut butter (do not use old-fashioned style or freshly ground)
3 tablespoons fresh lime juice
3 tablespoons soy sauce
½ teaspoon dried red pepper flakes
½ cup vegetable broth

10 ounces dried Japanese-style noodles (udon) or linguine pasta
8 ounces snow peas, halved

3 tablespoons vegetable oil
2 red bell peppers, thinly sliced
14 ounces firm tofu, cubed, drained well on paper towels

2 green onions, sliced (garnish)
3 tablespoons chopped fresh cilantro (garnish)

Finely chop garlic in processor. Scrape down sides of work bowl. Add peanut butter, lime juice, soy sauce and red pepper flakes. Process to blend ingredients. With machine running, slowly pour vegetable broth through feed tube and process until sauce is smooth.

Cook noodles in large amount of rapidly boiling salted water until just tender, but still firm to bite. Add snow peas during last 30 seconds. Drain noodles and snow peas in colander.

Meanwhile, heat oil in wok or heavy large skillet over high heat. Add bell peppers and stir-fry until just tender, about 2 minutes. Remove with slotted spoon. Add tofu and stir-fry until just beginning to brown, about 1 minute. Return bell peppers to skillet and stir until hot.

Remove skillet from heat. Add noodles, peas and peanut sauce. Mix to coat noodles and vegetables evenly. Transfer noodle mixture to platter. Garnish with green onions and cilantro and serve.

POPULAR PASTAS

There seems to be no limit to the inventiveness of Italian pasta makers. There are more shapes than stars in the sky, but here is a sample of some that might be readily available in your neighborhood.

CAPELLINI: "Fine hairs," the most delicate spaghetti.

FARFALLE: "Butterflies," the American version, often called "bows," is generally made with egg noodle dough, though the Italian is plain pasta.

FETTUCCINE: "Small ribbons," the famous noodle that has been responsible for the fortunes of numerous restaurants around the world.

FUSILLI: "Twists," long spaghetti twisted into a corkscrew shape.

LINGUINE: "Small tongues," really a spaghetti, but the shape of a narrow, thick noodle.

MAFALDE: Fairly broad noodles with ruffles on both sides.

MARUZZE: "Seashells," which come in several sizes all the way up to the giant shells that are served stuffed.

MOSTACCIOLI: These are called "small moustaches," though it's hard to imagine someone like Hercule Poirot sporting something that resembles any one of these.

PERCIATELLI: "Small, pierced" pasta, is about twice as thick as spaghetti and hollow.

SPAGHETTI: This, the most famous of all the pasta shapes, is a solid slender rod. The name means a length of cord or string.

VERMICELLI: "Little worms," very thin spaghetti.

ZITI: "Bridegrooms," large tubular macaroni.

Spinach Linguine with Goat Cheese

A sophisticated main course.

2 SERVINGS

3 tablespoons olive oil
1 bunch green onions, sliced
4 plum tomatoes, chopped
1 red bell pepper, chopped
6 oil-packed sun-dried tomatoes,
    drained, chopped
2 garlic cloves, minced
¼ teaspoon dried oregano, crumbled
1 tablespoon chopped fresh parsley
1 tablespoon chopped fresh basil or
    1 teaspoon dried, crumbled
Salt and pepper
8 ounces spinach linguine or
    spaghetti, freshly cooked
4 ounces soft goat cheese (such as
    Montrachet), sliced

Heat oil in heavy large skillet over medium heat. Add next 6 ingredients and sauté until onions are tender, about 15 minutes.

Stir in parsley and basil. Season with salt and pepper. Add pasta; toss thoroughly. Divide pasta between 2 plates. Top each with half of goat cheese.

Linguine with Arugula, Pine Nuts and Parmesan Cheese

6 SERVINGS

1 pound linguine

½ cup olive oil
4 ounces arugula, trimmed

1 cup freshly grated Parmesan cheese
    Salt and pepper
½ cup pine nuts, toasted
    Additional freshly grated
    Parmesan cheese

Cook linguine in large pot of boiling salted water until just tender but still firm to bite, stirring occasionally.

Meanwhile, heat oil in heavy large skillet over medium heat. Add arugula and stir until just wilted, about 30 seconds. Remove from heat.

Drain pasta and return to pot. Add arugula and toss well. Add 1 cup Parmesan and salt and pepper to taste; toss well. Transfer to bowl. Sprinkle with pine nuts. Serve immediately, passing additional Parmesan separately.

STOCKING THE PASTA PANTRY

With these basic staples on hand, several pasta meals can be stirred together without your even having to make a special trip to the market; other recipes require only the addition of one or two purchased fresh items.

IN THE CUPBOARD

Assorted dried pastas
Olive oil
Roasted red peppers packed in jars
Dried red pepper flakes
Capers
Canned anchovy fillets
Canned chicken broth
Bottled clam juice
Canned chickpeas (garbanzo beans) and other beans
Sun-dried tomatoes
Dried herbs
Canned Italian plum tomatoes
Walnuts
Onions
Garlic
Shallots

IN THE REFRIGERATOR OR FREEZER

Frozen vegetables (such as corn and peas)
Unsalted butter
Whipping cream
Parmesan and/or Romano cheese
Sliced prosciutto
Frozen scallops and shrimp
Sweet Italian sausage
Smoked turkey
At least one kind of cheese- or meat-filled pasta
Lemons
Imported brine-cured black olives

Pizza

MESQUITE-GRILLED PIZZA

MAKES ONE 14-INCH PIZZA

1 envelope dry yeast
¾ cup plus 2 tablespoons warm
   water (105°F to 115°F)
2 tablespoons olive oil
2½ cups (or more) bread flour
1 teaspoon salt

   Olive oil

1 cup prepared pizza sauce
¾ cup pitted black olives, halved
¼ cup pitted green olives, halved
12 ounces mozzarella cheese,
   shredded (about 3½ cups)
½ cup grated Parmesan cheese
⅓ pound mushrooms, sliced
½ green bell pepper, cut julienne
½ red bell pepper, cut julienne
1 tablespoon olive oil

Minced fresh herbs such as
   oregano, basil and rosemary
   (optional)
½ cup mesquite chips soaked in
   water 30 minutes and drained

Sprinkle yeast over warm water in small bowl; stir to dissolve. Let stand 5 minutes. Stir in 2 tablespoons oil. Mix 2½ cups flour and salt in processor using on/off turns. With machine running, pour yeast mixture through feed tube and process until combined, about 10 seconds. Knead dough on lightly floured surface until smooth and elastic, adding more flour to dough if sticky, about 5 minutes.

Brush large bowl with olive oil. Add dough, turning to coat entire surface. Cover and let rise in warm, draft-free area until doubled in volume, about 1½ hours. (*Can be prepared 1 day ahead. Punch dough down; cover and refrigerate. Bring to room temperature before continuing with recipe.*)

Prepare covered barbecue grill (medium-high heat). Brush 14-inch pizza pan with 1-inch-high sides with olive oil. Punch dough down and knead 2 minutes. Roll dough out on lightly floured surface to 16-inch round. Transfer to prepared pan. Spread sauce over dough; sprinkle with black and green olives. Top with both cheeses, then mushrooms and bell peppers. Drizzle with 1 tablespoon oil. Sprinkle with minced herbs if desired.

Add mesquite chips to fire. Open bottom barbecue vent. Place pizza on rack on lowest rung. Cover, leaving top vent half-open. Bake until crust is golden brown, checking occasionally, about 15 minutes. Serve immediately.

TWO-CHEESE PIZZA

Serve this deliciously different pizza as an appetizer or main course. You can make the crust as thick or thin as desired.

MAKES TWO 14-INCH PIZZAS

TOPPING

3 tablespoons olive oil
4 large onions, sliced

2 garlic cloves, minced
1½ tablespoons Dijon mustard
Pepper

DOUGH

1½ cups warm water (125°F to
   130°F)
1 package dry fast-rising yeast
1 tablespoon honey
1 teaspoon salt
3 tablespoons olive oil
4 cups (about) unbleached all
   purpose flour

Additional olive oil
1 cup crumbled feta cheese (about
   8 ounces)
3 cups packed shredded Havarti or
   Swiss cheese (about 12 ounces)
¾ cup sliced pitted Kalamata olives*
   (about 4 ounces)
1 tablespoon caraway seeds

FOR TOPPING: Heat olive oil in heavy large skillet over medium-high heat. Add onions and garlic and sauté until onions are golden brown, about 10 minutes. Remove from heat. Stir in mustard. Season with pepper. (*Can be prepared 1 day ahead. Cover and refrigerate. Let stand at room temperature before continuing.*)

FOR DOUGH: Combine first 4 ingredients in bowl. Stir until yeast dissolves. Mix in oil. Gradually add enough flour to form soft dough. Knead on lightly floured surface until smooth and elastic, adding more flour if sticky, about 8 minutes. Cover; let stand 30 minutes.

Preheat oven to 450°F. Oil two 16-inch-diameter pizza pans or heavy large cookie sheets. Divide dough in half. Roll each piece out to 12-inch round for thick crust or 14-inch round for thinner crust. Transfer to prepared pans. Spread half of onion mixture evenly over each pizza. Top each with half of feta, then half of Havarti. Sprinkle olives and caraway seeds over cheese. Bake until cheeses melt and crusts are golden brown, about 20 minutes. Let cool 5 minutes. Cut into wedges and serve.

Black, brine-cured olives available at Italian and Middle Eastern markets and specialty foods stores.

TRUTH IN LABELING

THE FOOD AND DRUG ADMINISTRATION recently took another step in its campaign for accurate food labeling. FDA officials cited several major food companies for misusing the phrase "no cholesterol" on labels for vegetable oil and peanut butter (two products that didn't contain cholesterol in the first place); and the word "fresh" on orange juice made from concentrate as well as on heat-processed pasta sauce. As a result of the FDA crackdown, the offending companies agreed to change the wording on labels.

Sandwiches

GRILLED FLANK STEAK, ONION AND BELL PEPPER SANDWICHES

These steak sandwiches are fast and satisfying. Serve them with ice-cold beer and sodas.

12 SERVINGS

3 cups dry red wine
3 cups chopped onion
2¼ cups soy sauce
¾ cup olive oil
8 large garlic cloves, chopped
1 tablespoon plus 1½ teaspoons dry mustard
1 tablespoon plus 1½ teaspoons ground ginger
4½ pounds flank steaks
6 large bell peppers (red, yellow and/or green), cut into ¾-inch-wide strips
3 large red onions, cut into ½-inch-thick rings

Grilled French Bread Rolls (see recipe)

Combine first 7 ingredients in large bowl. Divide steaks, bell peppers and red onions among large shallow pans. Pour marinade over. Turn to coat. Cover and refrigerate 3 to 6 hours.

Prepare barbecue (high heat). Drain steaks and vegetables. Grill steaks to desired degree of doneness, about 4 minutes per side for rare. Transfer to platter. Grill vegetables until beginning to brown, about 4 minutes per side. Slice steaks thinly across grain. Arrange steaks and vegetables on large platter. Serve with grilled rolls, allowing diners to assemble.

GRILLED FRENCH BREAD ROLLS

MAKES 18

¾ cup olive oil
6 garlic cloves, flattened

18 large French bread rolls
Freshly ground pepper

Heat olive oil in heavy medium skillet over medium-low heat. Add garlic and cook until light brown, about 4 minutes. Discard garlic.

Prepare barbecue (high heat). Split rolls in half horizontally. Brush cut surfaces with garlic oil. Sprinkle generously with pepper. Grill rolls, oiled side down, until golden brown. Serve hot or at room temperature.

GRILLED EGGPLANT AND FONTINA SANDWICHES

Serve hot corn on the cob as an easy accompaniment, then top off the meal with sliced fresh peaches and a plate of store-bought sugar cookies.

4 SERVINGS

½ cup olive oil
3 large garlic cloves, minced
1 large long eggplant (about 1½ pounds)
Salt

4 sourdough rolls (or any large

crusty rolls), split horizontally
6 ounces Fontina or mozzarella
  cheese, thinly sliced
2 ripe tomatoes, thinly sliced
  Thinly sliced red onion
  Fresh basil leaves

Combine oil and garlic in small bowl and let stand at room temperature at least 15 minutes. Slice unpeeled eggplant into ½-inch-thick rounds. Place rounds on rack. Sprinkle both sides of eggplant liberally with salt. Let drain at least 15 minutes. Rinse eggplant and dry with paper towels. Brush both sides of eggplant generously with garlic oil.

Prepare barbecue (medium heat). Grill eggplant until slightly charred on outside and tender inside, turning frequently and brushing with oil, about 15 minutes. Transfer to plate. Brush cut side of rolls with garlic oil. Grill rolls, cut side down, until toasted and warmed through. Dividing remaining ingredients evenly among sandwiches, place eggplant rounds, cheese, tomato slices and onion slices on bottom half of each roll. Top with fresh basil leaves and upper half of each roll and serve.

SANDWICH NICOISE

6 SERVINGS

2 large red bell peppers

1 8-inch round French or Italian
  bread loaf (about 1 pound)

⅓ cup olive oil
2 tablespoons red wine vinegar
1 tablespoon minced fresh basil or
  1 teaspoon dried, crumbled
2 garlic cloves, minced
6 anchovy fillets, rinsed, drained
4 eggs, hard boiled, sliced
2 medium tomatoes, sliced
1 6½-ounce can oil-packed tuna,
  drained
8 oil-cured black olives, halved,
  pitted
¼ cup minced fresh parsley
  Freshly ground pepper

Char bell peppers over gas flame or in broiler until blackened on all sides. Wrap in paper bag and let stand 10 minutes to steam. Peel and seed. Rinse peppers if necessary; pat dry.

Using long serrated knife, cut bread in half, forming top and bottom. Remove centers of each half, leaving 1-inch-thick bread shells.

Combine oil, vinegar, basil and garlic in small bowl. Brush inside of bread shells with oil mixture. Layer anchovies, eggs, bell peppers, tomatoes, tuna, olives and parsley on bottom half. Season with pepper. Cover with top half of bread and press. Wrap tightly in foil. Cover with 3- to 5-pound weight (such as cutting board topped with cans) and refrigerate 30 minutes. (*Can be prepared up to 6 hours ahead.*)

Cut sandwich into wedges. Pierce each wedge with long toothpick or bamboo skewer and serve.

Eggs & Cheese

Dairy dishes have been criticized of late for their high fat and cholesterol content. But rather than shunning them, take the approach that many of these recipes do, adding other elements to extend the rich ingredients. Don't pass up Wild Mushroom, Shallot and Gruyère Omelets or Leek and Potato Frittata. Enjoy them, within the limits imposed by your own dietary regimen—and always remembering the virtue of moderation.

WILD MUSHROOM, SHALLOT AND GRUYÈRE OMELETS

Offer with your favorite tossed green salad and some crusty bread.

2 SERVINGS;
CAN BE DOUBLED OR TRIPLED

4 tablespoons (½ stick) butter
4 ounces fresh wild mushrooms
such as shiitake or oyster,
trimmed, sliced
2 large shallots, minced
Salt and freshly ground pepper
1 tablespoon minced fresh parsley

6 eggs
4 teaspoons cold water
⅔ cup grated Gruyère cheese (about
2 ounces)
Minced fresh parsley (garnish)

Melt 1 tablespoon butter in heavy small skillet over medium heat. Add mushrooms and shallots and sauté until mushrooms are tender, about 2 minutes.

Season with salt and pepper. Remove from heat and mix in 1 tablespoon minced fresh parsley.

Beat 3 eggs and 2 teaspoons water in small bowl. Season with salt and pepper. Heat small omelet pan over medium-high heat. Add 1½ tablespoons butter and heat until foam begins to subside. Add egg mixture. Stir eggs with fork several times, drawing back of fork across bottom of pan. Lift edges of egg and let uncooked egg flow under until top is almost set. Spoon half of cheese, then half of mushroom mixture down center of the omelet. Fold omelet over filling in thirds and transfer to plate. Make second omelet with remaining eggs, water, salt and pepper, 1½ tablespoons butter, mushrooms and cheese. Garnish with parsley.

OMELETS MEXICANA

8 SERVINGS

1 pound ground beef
1 small onion, diced

1 teaspoon chili powder
1 teaspoon ground cumin
1 teaspoon dried oregano, crumbled
1 teaspoon garlic salt
½ green bell pepper, diced
½ red bell pepper, diced
½ cup prepared hot or mild salsa

16 eggs
8 tablespoons (about) vegetable oil
2⅔ cups grated cheddar
Sour cream

Cook beef and onion in heavy large skillet over medium heat until brown, stirring frequently, about 10 minutes. Pour off drippings. Add next 4 ingredients and cook 4 minutes, stirring frequently. Stir in bell peppers and salsa. (*Can be prepared 1 day ahead. Cover and refrigerate. Rewarm over low heat before continuing.*)

Whisk 2 eggs until well blended. Heat 1 tablespoon oil in nonstick skillet over medium-high heat. Pour eggs into skillet. Using spatula, lift edges of eggs as they cook, letting uncooked part run underneath until omelet is set. Spoon ½ cup meat filling over half of omelet. Sprinkle ⅓ cup cheese over. Slide out onto plate, folding omelet over filling. Keep warm. Repeat process for remaining 7 omelets, adding more oil to skillet as necessary. Top each with a dollop of sour cream.

CHILI SOUFFLÉ ROLL WITH CHUNKY TOMATO AND GREEN ONION SAUCE

Try this easy-to-make soufflé, with fillings of your own design, for other occasions.

6 SERVINGS

2 tablespoons vegetable oil
5 medium-size fresh Anaheim chilies* or canned green chilies (about 6 ounces), chopped
2 onions, thinly sliced
1 garlic clove, minced

½ cup all purpose flour
½ teaspoon ground cumin
¼ teaspoon chili powder
2 cups milk
4 large eggs, separated
   Salt and freshly ground pepper
1½ cups grated Monterey Jack cheese (about 5½ ounces)
1 tablespoon chopped fresh cilantro

Chunky Tomato and Green Onion Sauce (see recipe)
Cilantro sprigs (garnish)

Preheat oven to 325°F. Line 10x15-inch jellyroll pan with foil. Butter foil and lightly dust with flour.

Heat oil in heavy large skillet over medium-low heat. Add chilies, onions and garlic. Sauté until chilies and onions are tender, stirring occasionally, about 20 minutes. Transfer to bowl.

Place flour, cumin and chili powder in heavy medium saucepan. Gradually add milk, whisking until smooth. Cook over medium heat until thickened, stirring constantly, about 4 minutes. Beat egg yolks in medium bowl. Gradually whisk half of milk mixture into yolks. Return to remaining milk mixture in saucepan. Season with salt and pepper. Add ½ cup cheese and stir until melted, about 1 minute.

Place egg whites in large bowl and beat until stiff but not dry. Fold ¼ of whites into yolk mixture to lighten. Add chopped cilantro and fold in remaining whites. Pour soufflé mixture into prepared jellyroll pan, spreading evenly. Bake until puffed and golden brown, about 45 minutes.

Slide soufflé and foil onto work surface. Sprinkle soufflé with remaining 1 cup cheese. Spread chili mixture evenly over cheese, leaving ½-inch border on all sides. Starting from one long side, roll soufflé into tight cylinder using foil as aid. Cut into 1½-inch slices. Transfer to plates. Spoon warm Chunky Tomato and Green Onion Sauce over. Garnish with cilantro sprigs and serve.

Anaheim, also known as California,

chilies are available at Latin markets as well as specialty foods stores.

CHUNKY TOMATO AND GREEN ONION SAUCE

MAKES ABOUT 1½ CUPS

2 tablespoons corn oil
2 garlic cloves, finely chopped
1½ pounds plum tomatoes, cored, peeled, seeded, coarsely chopped
Salt and freshly ground pepper
Cayenne pepper
3 green onions, halved lengthwise, thinly sliced
2 tablespoons chopped fresh cilantro

Heat oil in heavy medium skillet over medium heat. Add garlic and cook until translucent, about 1 minute. Stir in tomatoes. Season with salt, pepper and cayenne pepper. Cook until slightly thickened and most of liquid evaporates, stirring occasionally, about 10 minutes. *(Can be prepared 1 day ahead. Chill.*

Reheat before continuing.) Stir in green onions and cilantro.

CREAMY SMOKED SALMON AND DILL TART

Purchased phyllo pastry is used here instead of a regular pie crust for quick and easy assembly. This tart is best when served at room temperature.

6 SERVINGS

5 frozen phyllo pastry sheets, thawed
3 tablespoons unsalted butter, melted

4 large egg yolks
1 tablespoon plus 1 teaspoon Dijon mustard
3 large eggs
1 cup half-and-half
1 cup whipping cream
6 ounces smoked salmon, chopped
4 green onions, chopped
¼ cup chopped fresh dill or 1

tablespoon dried dill weed
Salt and pepper
Dill sprigs (garnish)

Generously butter 9½-inch-diameter deep-dish pie plate. Place 1 phyllo sheet on work surface (cover remaining pieces with plastic wrap, then with clean, damp towel). Brush phyllo sheet with butter and fold in half lengthwise. Brush folded surface with butter. Cut in half crosswise. Place 1 phyllo rectangle, buttered side down, in prepared pie plate, covering bottom and letting pastry overhang 1 section of edge by ½ inch. Brush top of phyllo in pie plate with butter. Place second phyllo rectangle in pie plate, covering bottom and letting pastry overhang another section of edge by ½ inch; brush with butter. Repeat process with remaining, phyllo, making certain entire surface of edge is covered to form crust. Fold overhang under to form crust edge flush with edge of plate. Brush edges with butter. *(Can be prepared 4 hours ahead. Cover and refrigerate.)*

Preheat oven to 350°F. Whisk yolks and mustard in medium bowl to blend. Beat in eggs, half-and-half, cream, salmon, onions and chopped dill. Season to taste with salt and pepper. Pour into prepared crust. Bake until center is set, about 50 minutes. Transfer to rack. Cool. Garnish with dill sprigs and serve slightly warm or at room temperature.

LEEK AND POTATO FRITTATA

Steam some broccoli for a nutritious accompaniment, then pass a plate of purchased chocolate cupcakes for dessert.

4 SERVINGS

½ pound red potatoes (about 2 medium), halved

3 tablespoons unsalted butter
2 large leeks (white and light green parts only), thinly sliced

7 eggs
¾ teaspoon dried marjoram, crumbled

¼ teaspoon salt
¼ teaspoon pepper
¼ teaspoon ground nutmeg
4 ounces grated Gruyère or Swiss cheese

Chopped fresh parsley (optional garnish)

Cook potatoes in boiling salted water until just tender, about 12 minutes. Drain; cool slightly. Slice thinly.

Melt butter in heavy large skillet over low heat. Add leeks and cook until tender but not brown, stirring frequently, about 12 minutes. Remove skillet from heat. Add potatoes to leeks in skillet and toss to mix.

Preheat broiler. In medium bowl whisk eggs, marjoram, salt, pepper and nutmeg. Pour mixture over vegetables in skillet. Place skillet over low heat. Cover and cook until eggs are set around edges and center is barely set, about 10 minutes. Sprinkle cheese over frittata. Broil until cheese melts and begins to brown, about 1 minute.

Garnish frittata with parsley. Cut into wedges and serve from skillet.

SPINACH-HAM FRITTATA

Like all frittatas, this one is wonderfully versatile. Substitute one-half cup of almost any cooked vegetable for the spinach, and feel free to change the cheese to Swiss, Monterey Jack or mozzarella.

4 SERVINGS

3 tablespoons olive oil
1 garlic clove, minced
1 10-ounce package frozen leaf spinach, thawed, drained thoroughly, chopped
4 ounces ham, cut into ¼-inch dice

7 eggs
2 teaspoons Dijon mustard

4 ounces cheddar or Gruyère cheese, grated (about 1 cup)
Coarsely ground pepper

Heat oil in heavy medium nonstick skillet over low heat. Add garlic and sauté until fragrant, about 1 minute. Mix in spinach and diced ham.

Whisk eggs and mustard together in medium bowl. Pour eggs over spinach mixture in skillet. Stir gently to blend ingredients. Cover skillet and cook until eggs are almost set, about 8 minutes.

Meanwhile, preheat broiler. Sprinkle cheese over frittata. Broil until cheese melts and bubbles, about 1 minute. Sprinkle with pepper. Serve frittata warm or at room temperature.

HOTEL BENSON EGGS

This is a recipe reconstructed from a dish at an old hotel in Portland, Oregon.

4 SERVINGS

¼ cup (½ stick) unsalted butter
3 tablespoons flour
2 cups milk (do not use lowfat or nonfat)
1½ cups grated cheddar
8 slices Canadian bacon
1 tablespoon white wine vinegar
8 eggs
4 English muffins, halved, lightly toasted
Chopped fresh parsley

Melt butter in heavy medium saucepan over medium heat. Add flour and stir 2 minutes. Whisk in milk and cook until thickened, stirring constantly, about 4 minutes. Add cheese and stir until melted and well blended. Keep warm. *(Can be prepared 1 day ahead. Refrigerate. Rewarm over low heat before using.)*

Preheat oven to 300°F. Place bacon in single layer in baking pan. Bake until brown, about 10 minutes.

Place 2 inches salted water in large skillet. Add vinegar and bring to simmer. Break eggs 1 at a time into cup and slide into water. Poach until whites are set but yolks are still runny, about 4 minutes. Place 2 muffin halves on each of 4 plates. Top each with 1 slice Canadian bacon and 1 egg. Spoon some of sauce over. Sprinkle with parsley and serve.

Side Dishes

From Roasted Root Vegetables to Wild Mushroom and Bell Pepper Sauté, Couscous with Chick-Peas and Tomatoes to Rice Pilaf with Basil and Pine Nuts, the following pages offer up a veritable cornucopia of contemporary accompaniments. And if your palate is yearning for something different, compose a meal of several side dish recipes, letting them star on the table in their own right.

GRILLED SUMMER VEGETABLE MEDLEY

Try this recipe once, and you'll be hooked on the sweet and smoky flavors forever.

4 SERVINGS

3 tablespoons olive oil
2 garlic cloves, crushed
1½ teaspoons chopped fresh thyme
or 1 teaspoon dried, crumbled
1½ teaspoons chopped fresh sage or
1 teaspoon dried rubbed sage
1½ teaspoons chopped fresh
rosemary or 1 teaspoon dried,
crumbled
2 small Japanese eggplants, halved
lengthwise
2 small zucchini, halved lengthwise
2 small yellow crookneck squash,
halved lengthwise
4 ½-inch-thick slices red onion
1 red bell pepper, quartered, seeded
Salt and pepper

Combine first 5 ingredients in small bowl.

Place vegetables in baking pan and brush with oil mixture. Let marinate 2 hours.

Prepare barbecue (medium-high heat). Season vegetables with salt and pepper. Grill until just tender when pierced with tip of sharp knife, turning occasionally, about 8 minutes. Transfer vegetables to platter and serve warm or at room temperature.

BAKED FENNEL WITH GOAT CHEESE AND SAUSAGE

Rich, creamy and delicious. Serve as an accompaniment to roast veal.

6 SERVINGS

½ pound sweet Italian sausages, cut
into 1-inch pieces
1½ pounds fennel bulbs, trimmed
and cut lengthwise into ¼-inch-
wide slices
1 teaspoon fresh lemon juice

2 tablespoons (¼ stick) unsalted
butter
1 tablespoon olive oil
¼ teaspoon fennel seeds, crushed
½ cup water

2 tablespoons all purpose flour
1½ cups milk
Freshly grated nutmeg
Salt and pepper
¼ teaspoon minced fresh tarragon
or pinch of dried, crumbled
4 ounces fresh goat cheese (such as
Montrachet)
3 tablespoons freshly grated
Parmesan cheese

Cook sausages in heavy large skillet over medium heat until just cooked through and golden brown. Transfer to paper-towel-lined plate using slotted spoon and drain thoroughly.

Toss fennel with lemon juice in large bowl. Melt 1 tablespoon butter with oil in same skillet over medium heat. Add fennel and fennel seeds and sauté until fennel is translucent, about 3 minutes. Add ½ cup water. Cover and simmer until fennel is just tender, about 15 minutes. Transfer fennel to bowl using slotted spoon; reserve cooking liquid.

Melt remaining 1 tablespoon butter in heavy medium saucepan over medium heat. Add flour and stir 3 minutes. Remove pan from heat. Gradually whisk in milk and reserved fennel cooking liquid. Whisk over medium heat until sauce boils and thickens, about 5 minutes. Season with nutmeg, salt and pepper. Mix in fennel and tarragon. Transfer mixture to 6-cup shallow baking dish. Top with sausage and dollops of goat cheese. Sprinkle Parmesan over. *(Can be prepared 8 hours ahead. Cover and refrigerate. Let stand 1 hour at room temperature before baking.)*

Preheat oven to 375°F. Bake until knife pierces fennel easily and top is light brown, about 20 minutes.

TIMETABLE FOR GRILLED VEGETABLES

Vegetable	Minutes per side
Shiitake mushroom caps	1-2
Small zucchini, split lengthwise	3-4
Small yellow crookneck squash, split lengthwise	3-4
Small Italian or Japanese eggplant, split lengthwise	4-5
Onion slices (½ inch thick)	4-5
Red, yellow or green bell peppers, in halves or fourths	4-5
Russet potato slices (½ inch thick)	6-7

Cooking Notes

- All vegetables should be marinated or brushed with olive oil before grilling.

- Grill heat is usually uneven; to compensate, move vegetables around surface of grill throughout cooking.

- Turn slower-cooking vegetables at least four times during grilling.

- Your close attention is important—stay with the grill as vegetables cook.

- Times are approximate; foods were tested on an outdoor gas grill.

Wild Mushroom and Bell Pepper Sauté

6 SERVINGS

¼ cup (½ stick) butter
2 small red bell peppers, cut into bite-size triangles
2 small orange bell peppers, cut into bite-size triangles
8 ounces oyster mushrooms (cut large mushrooms into thirds)
Salt and pepper
3 tablespoons fresh tarragon leaves or 2 teaspoons dried, crumbled
3 ounces soft fresh pepper-coated goat cheese, crumbled

Melt butter in heavy large skillet over medium heat. Add peppers and sauté until tender, about 8 minutes. Stir in mushrooms. Season with salt and pepper. Sauté until golden brown, about 5 minutes. Mix in tarragon; cook 1 minute. Sprinkle with goat cheese and serve.

Mashed Potatoes with Green Onions and Parmesan

Pressing potatoes through a food mill or ricer gives them a fabulous texture. But they're just as delicious simply mashed.

2 SERVINGS; CAN BE DOUBLED OR TRIPLED

2 large russet potatoes (about 1¼ pounds), peeled, cut into chunks
2 tablespoons milk
2 tablespoons (¼ stick) butter

1 bunch green onions, chopped
⅔ cup freshly grated Parmesan cheese
Salt and freshly ground pepper

Cook potatoes in large pot of boiling water until tender. Drain well. Press through food mill or ricer into same pot or return to pot and mash. Mix in milk and 1½ tablespoons butter.

Melt remaining ½ tablespoon butter in heavy small skillet. Add green onions and sauté until wilted, about 1 minute. Add to potatoes. Add Parmesan and mix gently. Season with salt and freshly ground pepper and serve.

Roasted Root Vegetables

If baby vegetables are hard to find, cut large vegetables into one-inch pieces. Rutabaga and parsnips are good here, too.

6 SERVINGS

24 pearl onions, blanched 1 minute, peeled
18 baby turnips (unpeeled), trimmed, scrubbed
18 baby golden or red beets (unpeeled), trimmed, scrubbed
½ cup olive oil
Salt and pepper
¼ cup chopped fresh parsley
2 tablespoons chopped fresh thyme or 1 teaspoon dried, crumbled

Preheat oven to 375°F. Place onions, turnips and beets in large roasting pan. Pour oil over and turn vegetables to coat well. Season with salt and pepper. Roast until tender and beginning to brown, stirring occasionally, about 45 minutes. Transfer to serving platter. Sprinkle with parsley and thyme and serve.

SAUTÉ OF SPRING PEAS WITH TARRAGON

For a pretty, decorative touch, snip a V at one end of each snow pea.

8 SERVINGS

3 tablespoons unsalted butter
1½ pounds fresh peas, shelled, or
   1¾ cups frozen, thawed
8 ounces snow peas, trimmed
3 tablespoons fresh whole tarragon
   leaves
  Salt and freshly ground pepper

Melt butter in heavy large skillet over medium heat. Add peas and snow peas. Stir to coat. Cook until just tender, stirring occasionally, about 3 minutes. Stir in tarragon. Season with salt and pepper. Serve immediately.

COUSCOUS WITH CHICKPEAS AND TOMATOES

Offer this healthful Moroccan grain dish as an accompaniment to roasted chicken.

4 SERVINGS

1½ cups canned chicken broth
  2 tablespoons (¼ stick) butter
  1 cup couscous
  1 tomato, seeded, diced
  ½ cup drained canned chickpeas
    (garbanzo beans)
  ¼ cup raisins
  ¼ teaspoon ground cinnamon
  ¼ teaspoon dried basil, crumbled
  ¼ teaspoon dried thyme, crumbled
  Salt and pepper

Preheat oven to 350°F. Butter small baking dish. Bring chicken broth and butter to boil in heavy medium saucepan. Add couscous. Reduce heat to low. Cover and simmer until couscous is tender and has absorbed all liquid, about 5 minutes. Stir in tomato, chickpeas, raisins, cinnamon, basil and thyme.

Season with salt and pepper. Transfer mixture to baking dish. Cover and cook until baked through, about 15 minutes.

YOGURT MASHED POTATOES

A low-calorie recipe for the microwave.

4 SERVINGS

1¼ cups plain yogurt
  4 green onions, sliced
  ½ to 1 teaspoon curry powder
  2 pounds red potatoes, peeled, cut
    into eighths
  ¼ cup milk
  Salt and pepper
  Chopped fresh parsley (garnish)

Combine yogurt, green onions and curry powder in bowl. Place potatoes in microwave-safe dish. Add milk. Cover tightly and cook on high until potatoes are tender but not mushy, about 12 minutes. Remove from microwave. Add yogurt mixture and mash roughly. Season with salt and pepper. Garnish with parsley.

EAT YOUR VEGETABLES

Vegetables add color, texture, fiber, vitamins and minerals to the daily diet. They're also low in calories and act as roughage. So be sure to eat all your greens—they're perhaps the easiest way to a healthier you.

Keep a supply of cherry tomatoes and cut-up celery or carrot sticks in the fridge for afternoon snacks.

Steaming vegetables leaves much of their nutritional value intact without adding any calories. For a quick and easy flavor boost, add herbs, spices, wine or chicken stock to the water.

Steam vegetables and then puree for a fresh-tasting sauce for chicken or fish. Thin with appropriate low-salt stock if necessary. Roasted, pureed red bell peppers, with stock, also make a delicious sauce for chicken or fish.

Grill vegetables to add flavor. You can brush them with low-calorie bottled vinaigrette first, if desired. Corn, bell peppers, zucchini, onions and eggplant are vegetables that grill well.

Braise chopped vegetables in broth instead of sautéing them in butter.

Potatoes are low in calories and high in vitamins and minerals. Try a topping of buttermilk, yogurt or cottage cheese on your baked potato for a delicious but low-calorie alternative to butter or sour cream. Mashed potatoes instead of flour or cream can be used to thicken sauces. Also, toss quartered potatoes with just a little olive oil and some crumbled dried herbs, such as rosemary or thyme or even lemon peel, and oven-roast them until crisp and brown.

Asparagus is a rich source or beta carotene (the precursor of vitamin A), vitamin C and selenium—all possible cancer fighters. Look for firm stalks and tightly closed tips. Steam until crisp-tender and serve hot with a squeeze of lemon. Or chill and serve as a salad with oil and vinegar dressing.

Broccoli has beta carotene, vitamin C and potassium. This low-calorie, fat-free member of the cabbage family, when steamed just until tender, is delicious in stir-fry dishes and salads.

Cabbage is high in vitamin C, potassium and fiber, and low in calories (only 30 per cup of cooked). Use this versatile vegetable in coleslaw or shredded in soup; or wrap blanched leaves around savory fillings before steaming or baking to seal in natural juices.

EAT YOUR VEGETABLES

Spinach, kale, chard, mustard and collard greens are among the most nutrient-rich vegetables. Bright color and firm leaves indicate freshness. Clean these carefully since they tend to be gritty. Also trim away tough stems. Braised or sautéed, they are delicious on their own or added to soups, stews and omelets. They also make a colorful filling for other vegetables like tomato halves or artichoke bottoms.

Hubbard, kabocha, acorn and butternut are among the winter squashes richest in vitamin C, beta carotene and fiber. Buy squash that feels heavy for its size and has a firm and blemish-free rind. To bake, cut squash in half and place cut side down in pan, adding ½ inch of water. Or simply pierce a few holes in the squash and microwave whole. When cooked and mashed, these make a delicious alternative to more caloric sweet potatoes.

Tomatoes are a powerhouse of vitamins A and C. For best flavor, store at room temperature a few days until ripe and fragrant. Chopped tomatoes mixed with herbs, garlic, vinegar and just a dash of oil makes a delicious relish for crusty bread or topping for pasta. Tomato-based salsas can be used for healthful sauces with meat, fish, cooked eggs and potatoes. And fresh seeded tomatoes add color and nutrition to meat loaf, sauces, or casseroles. Halve a large tomato and fill it with scrambled eggs, rice or succotash.

Peas, either fresh or frozen, are loaded with vitamins A and C. They have no fat and are a good source of cholesterol-lowering fiber. Snow peas, also called Chinese peas, and sugar snap peas are eaten with the pod. These cook in a minute or less and add color and crunch to stir-fry dishes. Add cooked peas to potato or pasta salad for extra color and nutrition.

LEMON-SCENTED SAFFRON RICE

This creamy rice, fragrant with lemon, makes a nice accompaniment to the subtly flavored veal. If you like, pack the rice into half-cup custard cups and unmold onto the serving plates. Garnish with additional snipped chives, if desired.

8 SERVINGS

3 tablespoons unsalted butter
3 large shallots, thinly sliced
  Pinch (generous) of saffron threads
1½ cups Arborio* or other short-grain rice
3 cups chicken stock or canned low-salt broth
3 tablespoons fresh lemon juice
2 tablespoons chopped lemon peel
1 large bunch chives, chopped (about ½ cup)
  Salt and freshly cracked white pepper

Melt butter in heavy large saucepan over medium heat. Add shallots and saffron and cook 3 minutes, stirring occasionally. Add rice and stir to coat. Add stock and lemon juice; bring to boil. Reduce heat to low, stir and cover. Let simmer until creamy and tender, stirring vigorously every 10 minutes, 20 to 25 minutes. Add lemon peel and chives. Season with salt and pepper. Stir vigorously until well combined.

*Arborio, an Italian short-grain rice, is available at Italian markets as well as many specialty foods stores.

RICE PILAF WITH BASIL AND PINE NUTS

2 SERVINGS;
CAN BE DOUBLED OR TRIPLED

1 14½-ounce can chicken broth
1½ tablespoons olive oil
½ large onion, chopped
1 cup long-grain rice
⅓ cup chopped fresh basil or

1½ teaspoons dried, crumbled
¼ cup toasted pine nuts
  Salt and pepper

Bring broth to simmer in small saucepan. Reduce heat to low and keep warm. Meanwhile, heat oil in another heavy small saucepan over medium heat. Add onion and sauté until translucent, about 6 minutes. Add rice and stir 1 minute. Add broth and bring to boil. Reduce heat to low. Cover and cook until broth is absorbed and rice is tender, about 20 minutes. Stir basil and toasted pine nuts into rice. Season with salt and pepper and serve hot.

WILD MUSHROOM AND ORZO "RISOTTO"

Orzo—rice-shaped pasta—is easier to find than Arborio rice (the traditional ingredient in risotto) and makes a delicious risotto-style side dish.

6 SERVINGS

⅞ to 1 ounce dried porcini mushrooms*

1½ cups hot water

3 tablespoons olive oil
1 medium onion, chopped
2 cups orzo

4 cups canned low-salt chicken broth

½ cup freshly grated Parmesan
   cheese (about 1¼ ounces)
Salt and freshly ground pepper
Minced fresh parsley (garnish)

Rinse mushrooms briefly with cold water. Place in small bowl. Add 1½ cups hot water and let soak until softened, about 30 minutes. Drain mushrooms, reserving soaking liquid. Squeeze mushrooms and chop.

Heat oil in heavy medium saucepan over medium heat. Add onion and sauté until tender, about 8 minutes. Add orzo and stir until coated with oil. Mix in chopped mushrooms.

Meanwhile, combine 4 cups broth and mushroom soaking liquid in another medium saucepan. Bring to simmer. Reduce heat to low and keep hot.

Add 1 cup liquid to orzo, adjust heat so liquid simmers slowly and cook until orzo absorbs liquid, stirring occasionally. Continue adding liquid 1 cup at a time, simmering until each addition is absorbed before adding next and stirring occasionally until orzo is just tender and liquid is creamy, about 30 minutes. Stir in Parmesan. Season with salt and pepper. Garnish with parsley.

Porcini are available at Italian markets and specialty foods stores.

BENEFICIAL GRAINS

Grains are hearty, low-cost sources of fiber, protein and essential vitamins and minerals. Just remember that the protein is incomplete. To get the full benefit of protein, pair grains with a food that has complementary proteins, such as meat, poultry or fish (or for vegetarians, tofu, dairy products, beans or nuts).

Whole brown rice is the most nutritious rice available. Called "whole" because only the indigestible hull has been removed, this grain is a good source of fiber, calcium, B vitamins, iron and phosphorous. Removing the bran and germ to produce polished or white rice also removes most of the food value. To partially replace that loss, white rice is usually enriched (coated with some vitamins and minerals). White rice should never be rinsed before use or that enrichment is lost. Use cooked rice to thicken soups or bind meatballs. Or add chopped vegetables and vinaigrette dressing to cold cooked rice for a healthful salad.

Wild rice is the seed of grass native to the Great Lakes region. Indians of the area still harvest this protein-rich food by hand, though in recent years commercial cultivation has begun.

Wild rice is a good source of such nutrients as phosphorus, magnesium, potassium, zinc and the essential amino acid lysine.

Moreover, it's low in calories and virtually fat-free, with a hearty flavor and texture. Wild rice cooks for almost an hour in most cases, but once prepared, holds a week under refrigeration. Use as a side dish, in stuffings, casseroles, or add it to pancake batter.

Whole grain oats, called groats, are a fine source of B vitamins, vitamin E, calcium and iron. In addition, these oats contain water-soluble fiber, which may aid in reducing blood cholesterol levels. Whole grain oats are sold in several forms—old-fashioned rolled, quick-cooking and steel-cut—but all have been only minimally processed, so most of their nutritional and fiber levels are retained. Try adding oats instead of breadcrumbs to your next meat loaf. Use a cup of finely ground oats in home-baked bread for a loaf that stays fresh and moist longer.

Wheat berries—unprocessed whole wheat—are low in calories, high in protein, carbohydrates, B vitamins and seven essential amino acids (protein building blocks). Wheat berries must be presoaked and precooked before being used in recipes, but they add a delicious flavor and texture to all kinds of breads, stews and salads.

BENEFICIAL GRAINS

Bulgur—wheat berries that have been steamed, parched and cracked—retains most of its protein, calcium, B vitamins and minerals despite being partially processed. It is a fast-cooking grain with a pleasant, nutty flavor, and can be used in many of the same ways as rice: in pilafs, salads, casseroles.

One of the oldest grains, millet is rich in protein, phosphorus, iron and calcium. Usually found in natural foods stores, the tiny seeds have a long shelf life when stored airtight. Millet for human consumption is hulled; the unhulled variety is commonly used for birdseed. Cook this grain like rice, using about ½ cup millet to 1¼ cups water or broth. For extra flavor, toast the seeds first in a dry skillet. Millet also makes a tasty addition to yeast breads.

Quinoa (pronounced keen-wah) is an ancient grain from South America that is fast building a following stateside. Quinoa is a high-quality source of iron and essential amino acids and rivals milk for calcium content. It cooks in only about 15 minutes but should be rinsed well first. Serve quinoa as a side dish like rice, enhanced with herbs, mushrooms or onions, and add quinoa to soups for body and nutrition.

Breads

It seems as if the more contemporary our tastes become, the more we actually favor old-fashioned, rustic breads like the raisin-studded Prairie Rye, cornmeal-and-molasses Quick Anadama, and Cinnamon Wheat Bread with Apricots and Dates featured on the following pages. And with good reason: They're flavorful, healthy, and—an always-important factor in these hectic modern times—surprisingly easy to make.

PRAIRIE RYE BREAD

A light raisin-rye that's great for toast.

MAKES 2 LOAVES

1 cup raisins
  Boiling water

3 cups warm water (125°F to
  130°F)
½ cup yellow cornmeal
⅓ cup unsulfured molasses
2 packages dry fast-rising yeast
2 tablespoons unsalted butter,
  melted, room temperature
2¼ teaspoons salt
1 teaspoon sugar
2 cups rye flour
2 teaspoons caraway seeds
6 cups (about) unbleached all
  purpose flour

  Additional cornmeal

¼ cup cold water
2 tablespoons cornstarch
  Additional caraway seeds
  (optional)

Place raisins in small bowl. Add enough boiling water to just cover raisins. Let stand until raisins are plump, about 20 minutes. Drain well.

Combine 3 cups warm water, cornmeal, molasses, yeast, butter, salt and sugar in large bowl. Stir until yeast dissolves. Mix in rye flour and 2 teaspoons caraway seeds. Gradually add enough all purpose flour to form soft dough. Knead dough on lightly floured surface until almost smooth, adding more all purpose flour if sticky, about 4 minutes. Pat dough out on floured surface to large rectangle. Spread raisins over dough. Fold dough, enclosing raisins completely. Continue kneading dough until elastic, adding more all purpose flour if sticky, about 5 minutes. Grease large bowl. Place dough in bowl, turning to coat completely. Cover with plastic and let dough rest 15 minutes.

Sprinkle heavy large baking sheet generously with cornmeal. Knead dough on lightly floured surface 1 minute. Divide dough in half. Roll 1 piece out to 12x6-inch rectangle. Starting at 1 long side, roll up dough jellyroll style. Pinch long edge to seal. Place loaf seam side down on prepared cookie sheet. Repeat with second dough piece. Cover breads with clean towel. Let rise in warm, draft-free area until almost doubled in volume, about 30 minutes.

Preheat oven to 350°F. Combine ¼ cup cold water and cornstarch in small bowl for glaze. Brush each loaf with glaze. Sprinkle each with caraway seeds if desired. Bake until crusts are firm and brown and breads sound hollow when tapped on bottom, about 45 minutes. Transfer to rack and cool.

CINNAMON WHEAT BREAD WITH APRICOTS AND DATES

MAKE 2 LOAVES

¾ cup chopped dried apricots
½ cup chopped pitted dates

1½ cups warm water (125°F to
  130°F)

½ cup (1 stick) unsalted butter, melted, cooled to room temperature
½ cup honey
2 egg whites
2 packages dry fast-rising yeast
2 teaspoons salt
3 cups whole wheat flour
⅓ cup finely chopped toasted walnuts
3 teaspoons ground cinnamon
3 cups (about) unbleached all purpose flour

Combine apricots and dates in small saucepan. Add enough water to saucepan to just cover fruit. Bring to boil; remove from heat. Let fruit stand 5 minutes. Drain well.

Mix 1½ cups warm water with next 5 ingredients in bowl. Stir until yeast dissolves. Mix in whole wheat flour, walnuts and 1 teaspoon cinnamon. Gradually add enough all purpose flour to form soft dough. Knead dough on lightly floured surface until smooth and elastic, adding more flour if sticky, about 8 minutes. Cover with towel and let rest 20 minutes.

Grease two 9x5-inch loaf pans. Form dough into 1-inch-thick oval. Place fruit mixture atop dough. Fold dough over fruit, enclosing fruit completely. Knead on lightly floured surface until fruit is incorporated into dough. Divide dough in half. Flatten 1 piece into 10x5-inch rectangle. Sprinkle with 1 teaspoon cinnamon. Roll up dough jellyroll style, starting at 1 long side. Tuck in ends. Place in prepared pan, seam side down. Repeat with remaining dough and 1 teaspoon cinnamon. Cover breads with towel and let rise in warm, draft-free area until almost doubled in volume, about 40 minutes.

Preheat oven to 375°F. Using sharp knife, cut 3 diagonal slashes in top of each loaf. Bake until golden brown and breads sound hollow when tapped on bottom, about 45 minutes. Cool in pans 5 minutes. Turn loaves out onto racks and cool completely.

GRILLED CHAPATI

MAKES 16

1⅓ cups whole wheat flour
⅔ cup all purpose flour
⅔ cup plus 1 tablespoon water

Combine whole wheat and all purpose flours in medium bowl. Gradually add water, stirring until mixture forms crumbly dough. Turn out onto work surface and knead until smooth, about 4 minutes. Form into 8-inch-long log. Wrap in plastic and refrigerate 1 hour.

Place dough log on lightly floured work surface. Cut into sixteen ½-inch slices. Roll 1 slice into 5-inch round (keep remainder covered with plastic). Repeat with remaining dough pieces, stacking rolled rounds between sheets of plastic wrap. (*Can be prepared 1 day ahead. Wrap tightly and refrigerate.*)

Prepare barbecue (medium-high heat). Remove dough rounds from plastic and grill until puffed and dry, about 1 minute per side. Serve warm.

LOW CHOLESTEROL CINNAMON ROLLS

MAKES 10 ROLLS

1 large russet potato, peeled

1 envelope dry yeast
½ teaspoon sugar
½ cup warm water (105°F to 115°F)

½ cup evaporated milk
¼ cup honey
3 tablespoons vegetable oil
1 teaspoon salt
5 cups (about) unbleached all purpose flour

2 egg whites, beaten to blend
1¼ cups firmly packed dark brown sugar

1 cup raisins
2 teaspoons ground cinnamon
Vegetable oil

Cook potato in medium saucepan of boiling water until tender, about 30 minutes. Drain, reserving ¾ cup cooking liquid. Mash potato and transfer 1 cup to large bowl, reserving remainder for another use. Mix ¾ cup cooking liquid into potato. Cool to lukewarm.

Sprinkle yeast and sugar over ½ cup warm water in small bowl; stir to dissolve. Let yeast mixture stand until foamy, about 10 minutes. Add yeast to mashed potato mixture.

Add milk, honey, 3 tablespoons oil and salt to potato mixture. Stir in enough flour, 1 cup at a time, to form soft dough. Knead dough on lightly floured surface until smooth and elastic, adding more flour if dough is sticky, about 5 minutes. Let dough rest on floured work surface 20 minutes. Gently punch dough down.

Grease large bowl. Add dough, turning to coat entire surface. Cover bowl. Let dough rise in warm area until doubled in volume, about 40 minutes.

Grease large cookie sheet. Gently punch dough down. Roll dough out on lightly floured surface to 20x15-inch rectangle. Brush dough with egg whites. Mix brown sugar, raisins and cinnamon in medium bowl. Spread sugar mixture over dough, leaving 1-inch border on all sides. Starting at 1 long side, roll dough up jellyroll fashion to form cylinder. Pinch seam to seal. Cut cylinder into 2-inch-wide pieces. Arrange rolls on prepared sheet, placing cut side up and spacing 2 inches apart. Brush rolls with vegetable oil. Let cinnamon rolls rise until doubled in volume, about 35 minutes.

Preheat oven to 350°F. Bake rolls until golden brown, about 30 minutes. Cool slightly in pan on rack. Serve warm or at room temperature.

SESAME AND SUNFLOWER WHOLE WHEAT BREAD

This recipe can easily be doubled.

MAKES 2 LOAVES

2 cups whole wheat flour

1 envelope dry yeast

1½ cups milk

¼ cup honey

1 tablespoon sesame or vegetable oil

1 egg, separated

½ cup cracked wheat*

2 teaspoons salt

1¾ cups (about) unbleached all purpose flour

½ cup salted shelled sunflower seeds

2½ tablespoons sesame seeds

1 tablespoon water

2 teaspoons chopped pecans

2 teaspoons rolled oats

2 teaspoons caraway seeds

2 teaspoons fennel seeds

2 teaspoons poppy seeds

2 teaspoons sesame seeds

Combine 1½ cups whole wheat flour and yeast in large bowl. Heat milk, honey and sesame oil in heavy large saucepan over medium heat to 115°F, stirring occasionally. Remove saucepan from heat. Add milk mixture to dry ingredients. Stir in egg yolk, remaining ½ cup whole wheat flour, cracked wheat and salt. Mix in enough all purpose flour, ½ cup at a time, to form soft, slightly sticky dough. Knead on lightly floured surface until smooth and elastic, adding more all purpose flour if very sticky, about 10 minutes.

Lightly oil large bowl. Add dough, turning to coat entire surface. Cover bowl with kitchen towel. Let dough rise in warm, draft-free area until doubled in volume, about 1¾ hours.

Grease cookie sheet. Punch dough down. Mix in sunflower seeds and 2½ tablespoons sesame seeds. Turn dough out onto lightly floured surface and knead until smooth. Divide dough in half. Pat each half into 1½-inch-thick round. Place on prepared sheet. Cover and let rise in warm, draft-free area until amost doubled, about 1¼ hours.

Preheat oven to 375°F. Using sharp knife, cut ⅛-inch-deep, 1-inch-diameter circle in center of one round. Starting at outside of circle, cut ⅛-inch-deep slit to edge of loaf. Repeat 4 more times, spacing evenly apart and dividing bread into fifths. Repeat with second loaf. Beat egg white with 1 tablespoon water. Brush over loaves. Sprinkle pecans in center of each loaf. Sprinkle oats, caraway seeds, fennel seeds, poppy seeds and 2 teaspoons sesame seeds into divided spaces.

Bake until brown and hollow-sounding when tapped on bottom, about 50 minutes. Transfer to racks and cool slightly. Serve warm or at room temperature.

*Also called bulgur, available at natural foods stores and supermarkets.

Quick Anadama Bread

An especially easy baking powder version of the traditional yeast-leavened cornmeal and molasses bread. Buttermilk, instead of water, gives the loaf moistness and tang.

MAKES 1 LOAF

1¼ cups all purpose flour
1¼ cups whole wheat flour
½ cup yellow cornmeal
 2 teaspoons baking powder
¾ teaspoon salt
½ teaspoon baking soda
1⅓ cups buttermilk
⅓ cup dark molasses
¼ cup (½ stick) butter, melted
 1 egg
   Poppy seeds

Preheat oven to 350°F. Grease 9x5-inch glass loaf pan. Mix all purpose flour, whole wheat flour, yellow cornmeal, baking powder, salt and baking soda in large bowl. Combine buttermilk, dark molasses, butter and egg in another bowl and mix to blend. Add to dry ingredients and stir until just blended. Spoon into prepared loaf pan. Sprinkle with poppy seeds. Bake until loaf is springy to touch, about 1 hour. Cool in pan on rack 10 minutes. Turn out onto rack. Cool bread to room temperature. Cut into slices and serve.

Apricot-Nut Bread

MAKES 1 LOAF

1 cup dried apricots, chopped

1 cup sugar
1 cup quick-cooking oats
¾ cup whole wheat flour
¼ cup cake flour
2 teaspoons baking powder
½ teaspoon salt
½ teaspoon baking soda
½ cup orange juice concentrate
1 egg
2 tablespoons vegetable oil
1 cup chopped walnuts or pecans
   Powdered sugar

Preheat oven to 350°F. Grease 9x5x3-inch loaf pan. Place apricots in heavy small saucepan. Add enough water to pan to just cover apricots. Simmer until apricots are plump and water is absorbed, about 15 minutes. Cool.

Combine sugar and next 6 ingredients in large bowl. Stir in orange juice concentrate, egg and oil. Mix in walnuts and apricots. Transfer mixture to prepared pan. Bake until edges begin to brown and toothpick inserted into center comes out clean, about 1 hour. Cool in pan 15 minutes. Turn loaf out onto rack and cool completely. Sift powdered sugar over loaf. (*Can be prepared 1 day ahead. Wrap tightly with plastic wrap and store at room temperature.*)

Desserts

Nobody ever said a contemporary diet had to be boring. Case in point: the recipes in this chapter. Fruit stars on the 1990s dessert table, from Pears Poached in Red Wine to Summer Fruit Shortcake Pie. But still more modern recipes—from Bourbon Pecan Torte to White Chocolate and Orange Souffle—offer wondrous opportunities to yield to temptation. Go ahead: Indulge yourself, just a little!

Peaches and Raspberries in Spiced White Wine

8 SERVINGS

1 bottle (750 ml) Italian dry white wine, such as Pinot Bianco or Pinot Grigio
½ cup sugar
4 ¾x2-inch orange peel strips (orange part only)
3 cinnamon sticks

6 peaches
2 ½-pint baskets raspberries
Biscotti

Combine 1 cup wine, sugar, orange peel and cinnamon in small saucepan. Stir over low heat until sugar dissolves. Increase heat; simmer 15 minutes. Remove from heat; add remaining wine.

Blanch peaches in large pot of boiling water 20 seconds. Transfer to bowl of cold water, using slotted spoon. Drain. Pull off skin with small sharp knife. Slice peaches and transfer to large bowl. Add raspberries and wine mixture. Cover and refrigerate at least 1 hour. *(Can be prepared 6 hours ahead. Stir occasionally.)* Divide among glass goblets. Serve with biscotti.

Pears Poached in Red Wine

A recipe that's a year-round delight. In summer, when peaches are in season, they can be used instead of pears to create this light and sophisticated dessert.

8 SERVINGS

3 cups dry red wine
1 cup sugar
1 cinnamon stick, broken into 4 pieces
½ vanilla bean or 2 tablespoons vanilla
4 whole cloves
4 firm ripe pears, peeled

Bring red wine, sugar, cinnamon, vanilla and whole cloves to boil in heavy large saucepan. Add pears and simmer until tender but not mushy, turning occasionally, about 15 minutes. Transfer pears and syrup to large bowl. Refrigerate until well chilled, about 4 hours. *(Can be prepared 2 days ahead.)*

Cut pears lengthwise in half and remove cores. Starting ½ inch from stem end, make several lengthwise cuts in each pear half. Transfer pear halves to plates. Press gently on pears to fan slices. Serve pears with syrup.

Raspberry and Fig Gratin

4 SERVINGS

2 baskets fresh raspberries
6 fresh figs, quartered
8 ounces sour cream
½ cup firmly packed dark brown sugar
Mint sprigs (garnish)

Preheat broiler. Arrange raspberries and figs in 10-inch-diameter broilerproof baking dish. Stir sour cream until smooth;

spoon evenly over fruit. Sprinkle with brown sugar. Broil close to heat source until brown sugar melts and bubbles, about 4 minutes. Garnish with mint and serve warm.

BROILED FIGS WITH ORANGES AND SHERRY CREAM

6 SERVINGS

1 cup chilled whipping cream
3 tablespoons golden brown sugar
3 tablespoons cream sherry

6 oranges, peeled, white pith removed, sliced into rounds
Chopped fresh mint
12 fresh figs, halved lengthwise
Golden brown sugar
Cream sherry

Whip cream with 3 tablespoons brown sugar to soft peaks. Add 3 tablespoons sherry and beat to firm peaks. Cover and chill. (*Can be prepared 6 hours ahead.*)

Preheat broiler. Arrange oranges in ring around center of each plate. Top with mint. Arrange figs cut side up in broiler-proof pan. Sprinkle with brown sugar and sherry. Broil until sugar begins to caramelize. Mound cream in center of each plate. Top with figs and serve.

DRIED FRUIT STEWED WITH BROWN SUGAR AND VANILLA

This fruit keeps for several days in the refrigerator and is delicious for breakfast, too. Any dried fruit works well.

4 SERVINGS; CAN BE DOUBLED OR TRIPLED

4 cups water
½ cup firmly packed brown sugar
1 8-ounce package mixed dried fruit
4 orange slices
1 cinnamon stick
1 1½-inch piece vanilla bean, split lengthwise
Plain yogurt or sour cream
Ground cinnamon

Combine all ingredients except yogurt and ground cinnamon in heavy medium saucepan. Bring to boil, stirring until sugar dissolves. Reduce heat and simmer until fruit softens, stirring occasionally, about 20 minutes. Transfer fruit only to glass bowl, using slotted spoon. Boil liquid until reduced to 1 cup, returning liquid exuded from fruit to saucepan, about 10 minutes. Pour liquid over fruit, discarding orange slices. Serve warm, room temperature or chilled, topping with dollop of yogurt and dusting of cinnamon.

SPICED PUMPKIN AND PEAR TART

A deep-dish ginger crust adds a special twist to this delicious dessert.

8 SERVINGS

CRUST

1¾ cups unbleached all purpose flour
¼ cup sugar
¼ teaspoon salt
¾ cup (1½ sticks) chilled unsalted butter
2 egg yolks, beaten to blend
⅓ cup finely chopped crystallized ginger
1 teaspoon vanilla extract
5 tablespoons (about) cold water

PUMPKIN FILLING

2 large eggs
1 cup sugar
1 16-ounce can solid pack pumpkin
¼ cup whipping cream
¾ teaspoon ground ginger
¾ teaspoon ground coriander
½ teaspoon ground nutmeg
¼ teaspoon salt
¼ cup (½ stick) unsalted butter

1 lemon, halved
2 pears (about 12 ounces), peeled, halved, cored
2 teaspoons sugar
½ teaspoon ground cinnamon

¼ cup apricot jam
2 tablespoons brandy

FOR CRUST: Combine flour, sugar and salt in large bowl. Cut in butter with fingers or pastry blender until mixture resembles coarse meal. Mix in egg yolks, ginger and vanilla. Stir in enough water to bind. Gather dough into ball; flatten into disk. Wrap in plastic. Refrigerate 15 minutes. *(Can be prepared 1 day ahead. Let dough soften slightly before continuing.)*

Lightly butter 10-inch-diameter tart pan with removable bottom and 2-inch-high sides. Roll dough out on lightly floured surface to 14-inch round. Roll dough up on rolling pin and transfer to prepared tart pan. Press pastry into pan. Trim and finish edges. Refrigerate pastry 30 minutes.

Preheat oven to 375°F. Line pastry with foil or parchment and fill with dried beans or pie weights. Bake until edges are set, about 20 minutes. Remove beans and foil and continue baking until crust is golden brown, about 20 minutes. Cool crust completely.

FOR FILLING: Beat eggs and 1 cup sugar in large bowl to blend. Whisk in pumpkin, cream, ginger, coriander, nutmeg and salt. Melt butter in heavy small saucepan over medium-high heat. Stir butter until light brown, about 2 minutes. Whisk into pumpkin mixture. Pour filling into prepared crust.

Squeeze lemon over pears to prevent discoloration. Slice pears lengthwise into ¼-inch-thick slices. Place pear slices on top of filling in spoke-shaped design. Sprinkle pears with 2 teaspoons sugar and cinnamon. Bake tart until center no longer moves when pan is gently shaken, about 1 hour 15 minutes. Cool on rack 10 minutes.

Combine jam and brandy in heavy small saucepan. Stir over medium heat until jam is melted and smooth. Brush pears gently with glaze. Cool completely. (*Can be prepared 6 hours ahead.*)

Fresh Fruit Tart with Boysenberry Cream

Any colorful combination of seasonal fruit can be used to decorate this pretty dessert. The boysenberry filling is an American take on the usual vanilla cream.

8 SERVINGS

FILLING

1 large egg
2 large egg yolks
1 tablespoon cornstarch
2 teaspoons fresh lemon juice
1 ½-pint basket fresh boysenberries or 1⅓ cups frozen unsweetened boysenberries, thawed
½ cup sugar
¼ cup (½ stick) unsalted butter

CRUST

1¼ cups unbleached all purpose flour
¼ cup sugar
Pinch of salt
7 tablespoons cold unsalted butter, cut into small pieces
1 teaspoon grated lemon peel (yellow part only)
3 tablespoons fresh lemon juice

1 1-pint basket strawberries, stemmed, halved
1 ½-pint basket fresh raspberries
1 ½-pint basket fresh boysenberries or blackberries
1 large peach, cut into ½-inch-wide slices
5 tablespoons currant jelly

FOR FILLING: Beat egg and yolks in small bowl to blend. Dissolve cornstarch in lemon juice in small bowl. Mix into eggs. Purée berries and sugar in blender. Strain purée through fine sieve into medium saucepan. Add butter and bring to simmer over medium-high heat. Slowly whisk hot berry mixture into egg mixture. Return mixture to same saucepan and cook until filling is very thick and boils, whisking constantly, about 3 minutes. Transfer filling to small bowl. Press plastic wrap directly onto surface to prevent skin from forming; refrigerate at least 6 hours. (*Can be prepared 1 day ahead.*)

FOR CRUST: Blend flour, sugar and salt in processor. Add butter and lemon peel and process using on/off turns until coarse meal forms. Add lemon juice and process until moist clumps form. Gather into ball; flatten into disk. Wrap dough in plastic and refrigerate 45 minutes. (*Can be prepared 1 day ahead. Let soften slightly at room temperature before continuing.*)

Position rack in center of oven and preheat to 350°F. Roll dough out on lightly floured surface to ⅛-inch-thick round. Fold dough over rolling pin and transfer to 9x1-inch tart pan with removable bottom. Gently press dough into pan. Trim and finish edges. Chill 15 minutes. Line dough with foil and fill with dry beans or pie weights. Bake 15 minutes. Remove beans and foil and bake until crust is golden, about 20 minutes longer. Transfer crust to rack and cool.

Spread filling evenly in crust. Arrange strawberries, cut side down, in irregular pattern on filling. Fill in with raspberries and boysenberries. Tuck peach slices between berries. Stir currant jelly in heavy small saucepan over low heat until melted. Brush jelly over fruit to glaze. (*Can be prepared 3 hours ahead. Refrigerate.*)

GINGERED PEAR PIE WITH GOLDEN RAISINS

8 SERVINGS

¾ cup golden raisins
¼ cup plus 2 tablespoons minced crystallized ginger (about 2½ ounces)

3 pounds ripe medium pears (about 7), peeled, cored, sliced ½ inch thick
½ cup sugar
3 tablespoons butter, melted
2 tablespoons quick-cooking tapioca
1 tablespoon fresh lemon juice
1¼ teaspoons ground cinnamon
¼ teaspoon ground nutmeg
2 Buttermilk Pie Crust Dough disks (see recipe)

1 egg
2 tablespoons milk

Vanilla ice cream

Combine raisins and ginger in heavy small saucepan. Add just enough water to barely cover. Simmer over low heat until liquid is absorbed, about 15 minutes. Cool completely.

Position rack in lowest third of oven and preheat to 400°F. Combine pears and next 6 ingredients in bowl. Stir in raisin mixture. Roll out 1 pie crust disk on lightly floured surface to 13-inch round (about ⅛ inch thick). Roll up dough on rolling pin and transfer to 9-inch-diameter glass pie plate. Gently press into place. Trim edges, leaving ¼-inch overhang. Spoon pears into pan, mounding in center.

Roll out second crust disk on lightly floured surface to 13-inch-diameter round. Roll up on rolling pin and unroll over pie. Trim edges, leaving ¾-inch overhang. Fold overhang of top crust under edge of bottom crust. Pinch edges together to seal. Crimp edges to make decorative border. Gather and reroll scraps. Cut out decorative shapes. Beat egg with milk in small bowl for glaze. Brush top of pie with glaze. Arrange dough cutouts decoratively atop pie. Brush cutouts with glaze. Make several slashes in top crust so steam can escape.

Bake pie until crust is golden brown and juices bubble up through slashes, covering crust edges with foil if browning too quickly, about 1 hour. Serve warm with vanilla ice cream.

BUTTERMILK PIE CRUST DOUGH

MAKES ENOUGH FOR 2 CRUSTS

2½ cups unbleached all purpose flour
2 tablespoons sugar
1 teaspoon salt
½ cup (1 stick) chilled unsalted butter, diced
½ cup chilled solid vegetable shortening
¼ cup plus 2 tablespoons buttermilk

Combine flour, sugar and salt in large bowl. Add butter and shortening. Cut in using hands or pastry blender until mixture resembles coarse meal. Add buttermilk and stir with fork until moist clumps form. (Dough can also be prepared in processor. Using on/off turns, cut butter and shortening into dry ingredients until coarse meal forms. Add buttermilk and process just until moist clumps form). Press together to form dough. Divide dough in half. Gather dough into balls; flatten into disks. Wrap separately and chill 1 hour. *(Can be prepared ahead. Refrigerate 1 week or freeze 1 month. Let dough stand at room temperature to soften slightly before using.)*

DOUBLE-CRUST APPLE CIDER PIE

Old-time Yankee pie bakers lament the disappearance of good pie apples. But stalwart New England ingenuity wins out again. Adding a cider reduction to Granny Smith and Golden Delicious apples results in a pie that's a winner.

10 SERVINGS

CRUST

2½ cups all purpose flour
1 teaspoon salt
1 teaspoon sugar
½ cup (1 stick) chilled unsalted butter, cut into pieces
½ cup chilled solid vegetable shortening
1½ teaspoons cider vinegar
5 tablespoons (about) ice water

FILLING

2⅔ cups apple cider
2⅔ pounds Granny Smith apples (about 7), peeled, cored, sliced
12 ounces Golden Delicious apples (about 1½), peeled, cored, sliced
1 cup sugar
¼ cup all purpose flour
½ teaspoon ground cinnamon
¼ teaspoon ground mace
¼ teaspoon salt
4 teaspoons fresh lemon juice

3 tablespoons unsalted butter, cut into small pieces

FOR CRUST: Combine first 3 ingredients in processor. Add butter and shortening and process until mixture resembles coarse meal. Combine vinegar and 2 tablespoons ice water in small bowl. Add to flour mixture. With machine running, gradually add enough remaining water, 1 tablespoon at a time, to form moist clumps. Gather dough into 2 balls.

Flatten into disks. Wrap each disk in plastic. Chill 30 minutes. (*Can be prepared ahead. Refrigerate up to 2 days or freeze 1 month. Let dough soften slightly at room temperature before using.*)

FOR FILLING: Boil cider in heavy small saucepan until reduced to ⅔ cup, about 25 minutes. Cool. (*Can be prepared 2 days ahead. Cover and chill.*)

Position rack in lowest third of oven and preheat to 425°F. Combine all apples, sugar, flour, cinnamon, mace and salt in large bowl. Add reduced cider and lemon juice and toss well.

Roll out 1 pie crust disk on lightly floured surface to 14-inch-diameter round. Roll up dough on rolling pin and transfer to 10-inch-diameter pie plate. Gently press into place. Trim edges of crust, leaving ½-inch overhang. Spoon apples into crust-lined pan, mounding in center. Dot with butter. Roll out second disk on lightly floured surface to 13-inch-diameter round. Roll up on rolling pin and unroll over pie. Trim edges, leaving ¾-inch overhang. Fold overhang of top crust under edge of bottom crust. Pinch together to seal. Crimp edges to make decorative border. Cut several slashes in top crust to allow steam to escape.

Bake pie 25 minutes. Reduce oven temperature to 350°F. Continue baking until filling bubbles, covering edges with foil if browning too quickly, about 50 minutes longer. Cool. Serve pie slightly warm or at room temperature.

MODERN MINCE PIE

This dessert, long favored by the British at holiday time, originally contained minced meat along with the fruits and spices. This version, more suited to the nineties table, is meatless and brimming with apples, dried fruit and lots of spices.

8 SERVINGS

3½ pounds small pippin apples (about 7), peeled, cored, chopped
½ cup chopped pitted prunes
½ cup golden raisins
½ cup dried currants
½ cup firmly packed dark brown sugar
¼ cup unsulfured (light) molasses
¼ cup brandy
¼ cup orange juice
¼ cup (½ stick) unsalted butter, cut into pieces
2 tablespoons dark rum
1 tablespoon grated orange peel
1 teaspoon grated lemon peel
1 teaspoon ground cinnamon
¼ teaspoon ground cloves
¼ teaspoon ground allspice
¼ teaspoon ground nutmeg
Pinch of salt

2 Buttermilk Pie Crust Dough disks (see recipe)

Milk
Rum raisin ice cream (optional)

Combine first 17 ingredients in heavy large saucepan or Dutch oven. Cook over low heat until apples are very tender and mixture is thick, stirring occasionally, about 1½ hours. Cool filling completely. (*Can be prepared up to 1 week ahead. Cover and refrigerate.*)

Position rack in lowest third of oven and preheat to 400°F. Roll out 1 pie crust disk on lightly floured surface to 13-inch-diameter round (about ⅛ inch thick). Roll up dough on rolling pin and transfer to 9-inch-diameter glass pie plate. Gently press into place. Trim edges of crust, leaving ¾-inch overhang. Fold overhang under crust so that crust is flush with edge of pie pan. Crimp edges with fork to make decorative border. Spoon filling into crust-lined pan, gently pressing flat.

Roll out second disk on lightly floured surface to 13-inch round. Cut out about 28 three-inch leaves using cookie cutter. Press leaves lightly with tines of fork to form vein pattern. Brush bottom of 1 leaf with milk. Place leaf atop mince, overlapping crust slightly and pressing to adhere to crust. Continue placing leaves atop pie in concentric circles, overlapping edges slightly until top of pie is covered. Brush crust with milk. Bake until crust is golden brown and mince bubbles, about 40 minutes. Cool completely. Serve pie with rum raisin ice cream if desired.

TROPICAL LIME MOUSSE PIE
This Caribbean-inspired dessert is perfect after a spicy barbecue.

8 SERVINGS

CRUST
8 whole graham crackers
½ cup sweetened flaked coconut
7 tablespoons butter, melted

FILLING
¼ cup amber (gold) rum
1½ teaspoons unflavored gelatin
4 large eggs
1 cup sugar
⅔ cup fresh lime juice
3 tablespoons grated lime peel

1 cup chilled whipping cream

Sweetened flaked coconut, toasted

FOR CRUST: Preheat oven to 350°F. Process graham crackers in processor until finely ground. Add coconut and butter and pulse to blend. Press crumb mixture on bottom and 1¾ inches up sides of 8-inch-diameter springform pan. Bake until golden brown on edges, about 10 minutes. Cool completely.

FOR FILLING: Place rum in small bowl. Sprinkle gelatin over. Let stand 10 minutes to soften. Whisk eggs, sugar and lime juice in heavy small saucepan over medium-high heat until mixture thickens and just comes to boil, about 4 minutes. Remove from heat. Add gelatin mixture and stir until gelatin melts. Mix in 2 tablespoons lime peel. Refrigerate mixture until cold but not set, stirring occasionally, about 30 minutes.

Whip chilled cream until soft peaks form. Fold whipped cream into lime mixture. Pour filling into crust. Refrigerate until filling is set, about 3 hours. (*Can be prepared 1 day ahead.*)

Sprinkle pie with toasted coconut and remaining 1 tablespoon lime peel. Cut into wedges and serve.

SUMMER FRUIT SHORTCAKE PIE

This version of the classic American dessert isn't limited to berries alone. The short-cakelike crust is great with all fruits.

8 SERVINGS

CRUST

1 cup all purpose flour
¼ cup pecans, toasted
3 tablespoons firmly packed light brown sugar
1½ teaspoons baking powder
¼ teaspoon salt
¼ cup plus 1 tablespoon chilled unsalted butter
2 tablespoons milk

FILLING

½ cup sugar
2 tablespoons cornstarch
Pinch of salt
½ cup plus 2 tablespoons fresh orange juice
2 tablespoons fresh lemon juice
¼ cup Grand Marnier or other orange liqueur

6 cups mixed fruit, such as hulled strawberries, raspberries, sliced bananas, sliced pitted plums, blueberries, and cantaloupe or honeydew melon balls
Whipped cream or vanilla ice cream (optional)

FOR CRUST: Preheat oven to 425°F. Combine first 5 ingredients in processor and process until pecans are finely ground. Add butter and process using on/off turns until mixture resembles coarse meal. Add milk and pulse until large moist clumps form. Gather dough into ball. Knead dough on lightly floured surface until smooth. Roll dough out between 2 sheets of plastic wrap to 11-inch round. Remove top sheet of plastic. Invert dough into 9-inch-diameter pie pan. Remove plastic wrap. Crimp dough edges to make decorative border. Bake until crust is golden, about 14 minutes. Cool completely. (*Crust can be prepared up to 6 hours ahead.*)

FOR FILLING: Combine sugar, cornstarch and pinch of salt in heavy large saucepan. Gradually mix in orange juice and lemon juice. Stir constantly over medium heat until mixture thickens and boils 1 minute. Remove from heat and stir in Grand Marnier liqueur. Cool filling 10 minutes.

Place fruit in large bowl. Pour orange juice mixture over. Toss well to coat. Spoon fruit into crust, mounding in center. Refrigerate pie until fruit is set, about 30 minutes. (*Can be prepared 3 hours ahead.*) Serve with whipped cream or vanilla ice cream if desired.

FRUITFUL SUGGESTIONS

High in fiber and vitamins, fresh fruit is a must for any well-balanced diet. And its natural sweetness makes fruit the perfect healthful snack or dessert.

To benefit from extra vitamins and fiber, eat or prepare washed fruit with the peel intact whenever possible.

Use puréed fresh or frozen fruits, such as berries and apricots, for naturally sweet yet low-cal dessert sauces.

To add sweetness and flavor to cereals and plain yogurt, try fresh or dried fruit instead of processed sugar.

For a simple and quick jam that can be very low in added sugar: Cook diced fruit in a small amount of water, covered, until tender. Sprinkle sugar to taste and continue to cook, uncovered, until thick. Store in refrigerator.

Cook diced fruit—bananas, apples, pears or apricots—with hot breakfast cereal to provide sweetness and texture without adding processed sugar.

Purée frozen banana pieces with yogurt or lowfat milk and vanilla extract for a nutritious, rich-tasting "shake."

Fruit juice concentrates can be substituted for sugar in some recipes. Use apple juice concentrate in place of sugar to sweeten iced tea or yogurt.

Raw grated apple adds moisture to meat loaf without adding fat.

Toss diced bananas, apricots or melon with fresh lime juice and perhaps a dash of cayenne pepper or ground cumin for a speedy chutney that has no added salt or processed sugar.

Cantaloupe, papaya and large peach or nectarine halves make delicious "bowls" for chicken or seafood salads.

BAKING THE PERFECT PIE

The secret to the success of any pie begins with the crust. It should not only be delicious and flaky, but easy to work with as well. Like the adjoining recipe for buttermilk pie crust. It is light, tender and sturdy and a delightful complement to any filling.

Before prebaking a crust, freeze it until it is firm, about 15 minutes. Then it should be lined with waxed paper and filled with dried beans or pie weights to ensure that the crust keeps its shape. If beans or weights are not available, crumple a sheet of heavy-duty aluminum foil, punch a few holes in it, then spread it out and press into the contours of the crust. It should work equally well.

Always bake a pie in the lowest third of the oven for a crisp bottom crust.

To prevent the crust's edge from browning while the center of the pie bakes, cover the edge with foil. Cut a seven-inch-diameter circle from a large square piece of heavy-duty foil to make an easy-to-use shield.

Before serving, let the pie cool slightly to allow the filling to set.

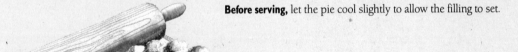

BOURBON PECAN TORTE WITH BROWN SUGAR WHIPPED CREAM

12 SERVINGS

TORTE

3¼ cups pecans (about 13 ounces)
¼ cup all purpose flour
2 teaspoons baking powder
¼ teaspoon ground nutmeg
½ teaspoon salt
6 eggs, separated
2 cups sugar
¼ cup bourbon whiskey

WHIPPED CREAM FROSTING

1¼ cups firmly packed golden brown sugar
¼ cup plus 2 tablespoons bourbon whiskey
3 cups chilled whipping cream

Pecan halves (for garnish)

FOR TORTE: Position rack in center of oven and preheat to 350°F. Butter and flour two 10-inch-diameter springform pans. Finely grind pecans in processor. Transfer pecans to medium bowl; mix in flour, baking powder, nutmeg and ¼ teaspoon salt. Using electric mixer, beat egg yolks and 1 cup sugar in large bowl until doubled in volume and slowly dissolving ribbon forms when beaters are lifted, about 5 minutes. Mix in ¼ cup bourbon. Fold into nut mixture.

Using electric mixer fitted with clean, dry beaters, beat egg whites and remaining ¼ teaspoon salt in another large bowl until soft peaks form. Gradually beat in remaining 1 cup sugar. Continue beating whites until stiff peaks form. Gently fold whites into pecan mixture in 2 additions.

Divide batter between prepared pans. Bake until toothpick inserted into center comes out clean, about 35 minutes. Cool in pans 15 minutes. Release pan sides; remove bottoms. Cool layers on rack. (*Can be prepared 1 day ahead. Cover tightly with plastic. Let stand at room temperature.*)

FOR FROSTING: Combine brown sugar and ¼ cup bourbon in large bowl. Stir until mixture is smooth. Gradually beat in whipping cream. Continue beating until stiff peaks form.

Place 1 torte layer on plate. Brush with 1 tablespoon bourbon. Spread about 2 cups frosting over torte. Top with second torte layer. Brush with remaining 1 tablespoon bourbon. Spread top and sides of torte with about 3½ cups frosting. Spoon remaining frosting into pastry bag fitted with large star tip. Pipe remaining frosting decoratively atop torte. Garnish with pecan halves. (*Torte can be prepared up to 2 hours ahead. Refrigerate.*)

GLAZED CHOCOLATE CARROT TORTE

8 TO 10 SERVINGS

3 slices whole wheat bread

2 cups whole blanched almonds (about 11 ounces)
1½ cups sugar

9 ounces bittersweet (not
   unsweetened) or semisweet
   chocolate, coarsely chopped
6 medium carrots, peeled, cut into
   2-inch lengths
6 eggs, room temperature
1 teaspoon vanilla extract
1 teaspoon almond extract
1 teaspoon instant espresso powder
   or instant coffee powder

Chocolate Glaze*

Position rack in center of oven and pre-heat to 350°F. Grease and flour a 12-cup bundt pan. Toast bread in oven until crisp and dry, about 15 minutes. Break bread into pieces and grind finely in processor. Measure ¾ cup crumbs.

Finely grind almonds, ½ cup sugar and ¾ cup breadcrumbs in processor, about 45 seconds. Transfer to large bowl. Process chocolate with ½ cup sugar until finely ground, about 30 seconds. Add to almond mixture. Insert fine shredder disk in processor. Stand carrots in feed tube. Shred, using firm pressure. Add to almond mixture.

Using electric mixer, beat eggs in large bowl until thick and foamy, about 3 minutes. Gradually add remaining ½ cup sugar, vanilla and almond extracts and espresso powder. Beat at high speed until slowly dissolving ribbon forms when beaters are lifted, about 7 minutes. Fold egg mixture into almond mixture in 3 additions. Transfer batter to prepared bundt pan. Bake until tester inserted near center comes out with just a few moist crumbs, about 65 minutes. Cool torte in pan 15 minutes. Turn out onto rack and cool.

Transfer torte to serving platter. Carefully spoon glaze over, allowing some to drip down sides. Let stand until glaze sets, about 1 hour. (*Can be prepared 8 hours ahead. Cover with cake dome; let stand at room temperature.*)

*CHOCOLATE GLAZE

MAKES ABOUT ¾ CUP

4 ounces bittersweet (not
   unsweetened) or semisweet
   chocolate, chopped
3 tablespoons water
2 tablespoons powdered sugar

Melt chocolate in top of double boiler over simmering water, stirring until smooth. Remove from over water. Mix in 3 tablespoons water. Sift powdered sugar over chocolate mixture and stir until blended and glaze is smooth.

Lemon Ice Torte with Strawberry-Rhubarb Sauce

This simple-to-prepare recipe makes more sauce than you'll need for the torte. Use the remainder as a breakfast fruit, topped with a dollop of plain yogurt.

8 SERVINGS

CRUST

3 cups blanched slivered almonds, toasted (about 12 ounces)
½ cup sugar
5 tablespoons margarine, melted
¼ teaspoon ground cinnamon
⅓ cup strawberry preserves
3 pints lemon or pineapple ice, sherbet or sorbet

SAUCE

1 cup sugar
½ cup water
1 vanilla bean, split lengthwise
1 20-ounce bag frozen unsweetened rhubarb
1 20-ounce bag frozen unsweetened strawberries
1 1-pint basket fresh strawberries
Fresh mint sprigs (garnish)

FOR CRUST: Combine almonds and sugar in processor and chop finely. Transfer to medium bowl. Combine margarine and cinnamon and mix into almonds. Transfer to 9-inch-diameter springform pan. Using plastic wrap as aid, press almond mixture firmly 2 inches up sides and then over bottom of pan. Freeze 15 minutes.

Preheat oven to 350°F. Place pan with crust on cookie sheet and bake 20 minutes. If crust sides slip, press back in place with back of fork. Transfer pan to rack and cool crust completely.

Melt strawberry preserves in heavy small saucepan. Pour into cooled crust and spread to cover bottom. Cool. Soften ice very slightly and spread in pan. Freeze until firm. (*Can be prepared 1 day ahead. Cover and freeze.*)

FOR SAUCE: Combine ½ cup sugar and ½ cup water in heavy medium saucepan. Scrape in seeds from vanilla bean; add pod. Simmer 5 minutes. Add remaining ½ cup sugar and stir to dissolve. Add rhubarb. Bring to boil, reduce heat, cover and simmer until rhubarb is tender, about 8 minutes. Add frozen strawberries and bring to simmer. Cool. Cover and refrigerate until well chilled. (*Can be prepared 1 day ahead.*)

Remove vanilla pod from sauce. Cut between crust and pan sides with small sharp knife. Remove pan sides. Spoon ½ cup sauce over center of torte. Mound fresh strawberries in center. Garnish with fresh mint sprigs. Cut torte into slices and serve with sauce.

Our Favorite Tiramisù

Layers of espresso-soaked pound cake and cream cheese custard come together with chocolate. Tiramisù means "pick-me-up" in Italian—and this certainly does.

8 SERVINGS

8 ounces semisweet chocolate
1 cup sugar
4 eggs yolks
1½ teaspoons vanilla
8 ounces cream cheese, cut into pieces, room temperature

1¾ cups chilled whipping cream

1 tablespoon instant espresso powder diluted in 1¼ cups hot water, cooled
1 12-ounce prepared pound cake, cut into 3½x1x½-inch strips

Finely chop chocolate in food processor. Set aside.

Mix sugar and egg yolks in processor 30 seconds. Add vanilla and process until pale yellow, about 1 minute. Add cheese in batches and blend until smooth. Transfer to medium bowl. Cover and chill 1 hour.

Beat whipping cream until stiff. Fold into cream cheese mixture. Cover and refrigerate until well chilled, about 1 hour. *(Can be prepared 2 days ahead.)*

Pour espresso into large shallow dish. Dip cake strips in espresso, turning to coat all sides lightly. Arrange on bottom of 10-cup shallow dish, smoothing with fingers to mold together. Sprinkle with half of chocolate. Top with chilled cheese. Sprinkle remaining chocolate over. Cover and refrigerate at least 2 hours. *(Can be prepared 1 day ahead.)*

Coconut Spice Cake

12 SERVINGS

CAKE

2 cups plus 3 tablespoons sifted unbleached all purpose flour
2 teaspoons baking powder
1 teaspoon ground ginger
¾ teaspoon baking soda
¾ teaspoon salt
¾ teaspoon ground cinnamon
1 cup (2 sticks) unsalted butter, room temperature
¾ cup sugar
2 eggs
½ cup plus 2 tablespoons light unsulfured molasses
2 tablespoons grated orange peel
1 teaspoon vanilla extract
¾ cup buttermilk
1 cup shredded sweetened coconut, toasted
½ cup diced crystallized ginger (about 2½ ounces)

ICING

8 ounces cream cheese, room
  temperature
½ cup (1 stick) unsalted butter,
  room temperature
2 tablespoons grated orange peel
1 teaspoon vanilla extract
1 1-pound box powdered sugar
⅓ cup minced crystallized ginger
  (scant 2 ounces)

1 cup shredded sweetened coconut,
  toasted
  Tropical fruit such as pineapple,
  papaya and mango, cut into bite-
  size pieces

FOR CAKE: Preheat oven to 350°F. Butter
two 9-inch-diameter cake pans with
1½-inch-high sides. Line bottoms with
parchment. Butter parchment; dust pans
with flour. Sift flour, baking powder,
ground ginger, baking soda, salt and
ground cinnamon into medium bowl.
Using electric mixer, cream unsalted butter and sugar in large bowl until fluffy.

Beat in eggs 1 at a time. Add unsulfured
molasses, grated orange peel and vanilla
extract and beat 1 minute at high speed
until well blended. Mix in dry ingredients alternately with buttermilk, beginning and ending with dry ingredients.
Fold in shredded coconut and crystallized ginger.

Divide batter between prepared
pans. Bake until cakes begin to pull away
from sides of pans, about 30 minutes.
Cool in pans on rack 5 minutes. Invert
cakes onto racks. Remove parchment
and cool completely.

FOR ICING: Using electric mixer, beat
cream cheese and butter until smooth.
Mix in orange peel and vanilla. Beat in
sugar. Mix in ginger.

Place 1 cake layer on platter, flat side
down. Spread with some of icing. Sprinkle
with ¾ cup coconut. Top with second
layer, flat side up. Spread remaining icing
over top and sides of cake. Arrange
remaining coconut around top edge of
cake. (*Can be prepared 1 day ahead. Chill*
until icing is set; wrap lightly with plastic
and refrigerate. Bring to room temperature.)
Place fruit around base of cake.

RASPBERRY AND COFFEE
TIRAMISU

An unexpected combination of ingredients
updates the classic Italian dessert. It is
presented in individual servings here, but
the ladyfingers, espresso and filling can be
layered in a large dish and offered with the
sauce on the side if you prefer.

6 SERVINGS

LADYFINGER ROUNDS

½ cup all purpose flour
½ teaspoon finely ground coffee
  (preferably espresso)
3 extra-large eggs, separated, room
  temperature
5 tablespoons sugar
½ teaspoon vanilla extract

  Powdered sugar

FILLING

3 tablespoons framboise eau-de-vie
(clear raspberry brandy)
1 tablespoon instant espresso
powder or instant coffee granules
2 8-ounce packages cream cheese
(preferably old-fashioned, low-salt
cream cheese), room temperature
⅔ cup powdered sugar
1 6-ounce basket raspberries or
1½ cups frozen unsweetened,
thawed, drained
¾ cup freshly brewed strong coffee
(preferably espresso), room
temperature
3 tablespoons sugar
Additional powdered sugar
Raspberry Sauce (see recipe)
Fresh mint (garnish)

FOR LADYFINGER ROUNDS: Preheat oven
to 350°F. Line 2 cookie sheets with
parchment. Mix flour and ground coffee
in small bowl. Using electric mixer, beat
egg yolks and 4 tablespoons sugar in
medium bowl until thick and slowly
dissolving ribbon forms when beaters are
lifted, about 4 minutes. Beat in vanilla.
Mix in dry ingredients (batter will be
thick). Using electric mixer fitted with
clean, dry beaters, beat egg whites until
thick and foamy. Add remaining 1 tablespoon sugar and beat until whites are
stiff but not dry. Fold into yolk mixture
in 2 additions.

Drop batter by rounded tablespoons
(8 per sheet) onto prepared sheets, spacing
evenly. Sift powdered sugar thickly over
rounds. Bake until rounds are golden
brown on edges, about 16 minutes. Cool
in pan on rack. Remove rounds from
parchment. (*Can be prepared 1 day ahead.
Store in single layer in airtight container.*)

FOR FILLING: Combine framboise
and instant espresso in small bowl. Stir
until espresso dissolves. Using electric
mixer, beat cream cheese and ⅔ cup
powdered sugar until light and fluffy. Beat
in coffee mixture. Fold in 1 cup raspberries. Let stand at room temperature.

Combine coffee and 3 tablespoons
sugar. Stir until sugar dissolves. Spoon 1
scant tablespoon coffee mixture over flat
side of 1 ladyfinger round. Place coffee
side up on plate. Spread ⅓ cup filling atop
round. Spoon 1 scant tablespoon coffee
mixture over flat side of second ladyfinger round. Place flat side down atop
filling. Sprinkle with powdered sugar.
Repeat with remaining ladyfinger rounds,
coffee, filling and powdered sugar. Spoon
Raspberry Sauce around desserts. Garnish
with remaining raspberries and fresh
mint and serve.

RASPBERRY SAUCE

MAKES ABOUT 1¼ CUPS

1 10-ounce package frozen
raspberries in syrup, thawed
2 tablespoons framboise eau-de-vie

Purée raspberries and syrup in processor.
Strain into small bowl to remove seeds.
Stir in eau-de-vie. (*Can be prepared
2 days ahead. Cover and refrigerate.*)

Peach Mousse in Pine Nut Cookie Baskets

The cookie baskets are a delicious and beautiful way to serve this refreshing mousse. Press the warm cookies over a custard cup to form the bowl shape. The recipe makes about 16 baskets, so you'll have enough if a few break. For an even easier dessert, purchase some waffle cone "dishes" from a local ice cream parlor and fill them with the mousse.

8 SERVINGS

COOKIE BASKETS

⅔ cup sugar
½ cup (1 stick) unsalted butter
3 tablespoons water
2 tablespoons plus 2 teaspoons
   light corn syrup
   Pinch of salt
1 cup blanched almonds, ground
½ cup pine nuts
6 tablespoons plus 2 teaspoons all
   purpose flour
¼ teaspoon ground cinnamon

PEACH MOUSSE

2 teaspoons dark rum
1 teaspoon vanilla extract
⅛ teaspoon almond extract
1¼ teaspoons unflavored gelatin
1 pound ripe peaches, peeled,
   pitted
3 tablespoons sugar
3 egg yolks

¾ cup chilled whipping cream
½ cup powdered sugar
½ teaspoon grated lemon peel

   Fresh mint sprigs (optional
   garnish)

FOR COOKIE BASKETS: Preheat oven to 350°F. Cut out sixteen 8-inch foil squares. Butter foil. Bring sugar, butter, 3 tablespoons water, corn syrup and salt to boil in heavy medium saucepan over medium-high heat, stirring constantly. Add almonds, pine nuts, flour and cinnamon and return to boil, stirring constantly. Remove from heat.

   Arrange 2 pieces of prepared foil on heavy large cookie sheet. Drop 1 rounded tablespoon of batter on each piece of foil. Bake until cookies are light brown, about 9 minutes. Remove from oven. Immediately turn one cookie over onto inverted custard cup and, using oven mitts as aid, press foil with cookie loosely around cup to form basket. Quickly repeat with second cookie and second custard cup. Let stand until cookies harden, about 5 minutes. Remove cookies from cups; carefully peel off foil. In batches of 2, repeat with remaining batter and foil squares. (*Can be prepared 2 days ahead. Store in airtight containers at room temperature.*)

   FOR MOUSSE: Combine rum, vanilla and almond extracts in small bowl. Sprinkle gelatin over and let soften at least 10 minutes. Purée peaches in processor. Pour into heavy medium saucepan. Add 3 tablespoons sugar and bring to simmer, stirring to dissolve sugar. Simmer 10 minutes. Whisk yolks in medium bowl to blend. Gradually whisk simmering purée into yolks. Return yolk mixture to same pan. Add gelatin mixture and stir over medium-low heat until candy thermometer registers 160°F, about 2 minutes. Transfer to large bowl and refrigerate until cold, stirring occasionally, about 40 minutes.

Whip cream with powdered sugar in large bowl until stiff peaks form. Whisk in lemon peel. Fold cream into peach mixture in 2 additions. (*Can be prepared 1 day ahead. Cover and refrigerate.*)

Arrange 1 cookie basket on each serving plate. Spoon mousse into baskets. Garnish with fresh mint and serve.

LEMON MERINGUE TERRINE
The combination of lemon and almond flavors is irresistible in this frozen dessert.

12 SERVINGS

TOASTED ALMOND MERINGUES

Powdered sugar

5 large egg whites, room temperature

½ teaspoon cream of tartar

1 cup sugar

½ teaspoon vanilla extract

¼ teaspoon almond extract

1¼ cups ground toasted blanched almonds (about 6 ounces)

1 tablespoon cornstarch

LEMON MOUSSE

4 large eggs

1 cup sugar

½ cup fresh lemon juice

½ cup whipping cream

2 tablespoons grated lemon peel

1¼ cups chilled whipping cream

1 teaspoon vanilla extract

1½ cups toasted sliced almonds

FOR MERINGUES: Preheat oven to 275°F. Line 2 large cookie sheets with foil. Butter foil and dust with powdered sugar. Cut a 12x4-inch cardboard rectangle. Using cardboard as guide, trace 2 rectangles on each prepared cookie sheet.

Using electric mixer, beat egg whites and cream of tartar in large bowl until soft peaks form. Gradually add sugar and beat until stiff and shiny. Beat in vanilla and almond extracts. Combine almonds and cornstarch in medium bowl. Gently fold nuts into egg whites in 2 additions. Spread 1¼ cups meringue over each marked rectangle on prepared sheets, filling rectangles completely. Bake until crisp and golden, about 1 hour. Cool meringues on sheets. Remove carefully and trim to 12x4 inches if necessary. (*Can be prepared 2 days ahead. Wrap tightly and store at room temperature.*)

FOR MOUSSE: Whisk eggs and sugar in large bowl until thick. Whisk in lemon juice. Scald ½ cup cream in heavy medium saucepan. Gradually whisk hot cream into egg mixture. Return mixture to saucepan and stir over medium heat until mixture thickens and leaves path on back of spoon when finger is drawn across, about 4 minutes. Do not boil. Pour into large bowl; mix in lemon peel. Press plastic onto surface of custard and refrigerate until cold, about 1 hour. Whip 1¼ cups chilled cream and vanilla extract in large bowl until firm peaks form. Fold cream into lemon mixture in 2 additions.

Place 1 meringue on platter. Spread with 1 generous cup mousse. Top with second meringue. Spread with 1 generous cup mousse. Top with third meringue. Spread with 1 generous cup mousse. Top with last meringue. Frost top and sides with remaining mousse. Press sliced almonds gently into mousse over top and sides of terrine. Freeze at least 4 hours. *(Can be prepared 4 days ahead. Wrap carefully. Keep frozen.)* Let stand at room temperature 15 minutes before serving.

WHITE CHOCOLATE AND ORANGE SOUFFLÉ

This moist orange-flavored soufflé is rich with white chocolate. Offer snifters of orange liqueur to sip alongside.

6 SERVINGS

½ cup whipping cream
¼ cup sugar
6 ounces imported white chocolate (such as Lindt), coarsely chopped
4 large egg yolks, room temperature
2 teaspoons grated orange peel
2 tablespoons Grand Marnier or other orange liqueur

3 large egg whites, room temperature
Pinch of cream of tartar
2 tablespoons sugar
2 ounces imported white chocolate (such as Lindt), coarsely chopped
Powdered sugar

Preheat oven to 350°F. Butter 6-cup soufflé dish. Sprinkle dish with sugar, tap out excess. Heat cream and ¼ cup sugar in heavy medium saucepan over medium heat, stirring until sugar dissolves. Add 6 ounces of chocolate and stir until chocolate dissolves. Whisk in yolks and orange peel. Cook until mixture thickens slightly, stirring constantly, about 5 minutes; do not boil. Whisk in Grand Marnier. Transfer mixture to large bowl.

Using electric mixer, beat egg whites and cream of tartar in large bowl until soft peaks form. Add 2 tablespoons sugar and beat until stiff peaks form. Mix 2 ounces chopped chocolate into warm egg yolk mixture. Fold in egg whites in 2 additions. Transfer mixture to prepared soufflé dish. Bake until soufflé is puffed and top is golden brown, about 35 minutes. Dust with powdered sugar and serve.

FROZEN BOYSENBERRY AND WHITE CHOCOLATE PARFAIT

Begin preparing this delicious dessert at least one day ahead.

6 SERVINGS

PARFAIT

1 16-ounce bag frozen
   boysenberries or blackberries,
   thawed
¼ cup sugar
1 tablespoon crème de cassis or
   other berry-flavored liqueur
½ teaspoon fresh lemon juice

¾ cup sugar
¼ cup water
6 large egg yolks
3 ounces imported white chocolate
   (such as Lindt), chopped, melted
2 teaspoons vanilla extract
1⅓ cups chilled whipping cream

SAUCE

1 16-ounce bag frozen boysenberries
   or blackberries, thawed
¼ cup sugar
2 tablespoons crème de cassis or
   other berry-flavored liqueur

Fresh boysenberries, blackberries
or strawberries (garnish)
Fresh mint sprigs (garnish)

FOR PARFAIT: Line 9x5-inch loaf pan with plastic wrap. Purée berries and ¼ cup sugar in blender until just smooth. Strain. Measure 1⅓ cups purée and place in heavy small saucepan. (Reserve any remaining purée for sauce.) Simmer 1⅓ cups purée over medium heat until reduced to scant 1 cup, stirring occasionally, about 8 minutes. Transfer to bowl and chill 30 minutes. Stir in cassis and lemon juice. Refrigerate reduced purée until ready to use.

Combine ¾ cup sugar, water and yolks in medium metal bowl. Set bowl over saucepan of simmering water. Using hand-held electric mixer, beat yolk mixture until it registers 140°F on candy thermometer, occasionally scraping down sides of bowl, about 5 minutes. Continue cooking 3 minutes, beating constantly. Remove from over water. Add warm melted chocolate and vanilla and beat until cool. Beat whipping cream in another large bowl to stiff peaks. Gently mix ¼ of cream into chocolate mixture. Fold in remaining whipped cream.

Transfer 1⅓ cups chocolate mixture to medium bowl. Fold in reduced berry purée. Fill prepared loaf pan with ⅓ of remaining chocolate mixture. Cover with berry-chocolate mixture. Top with remaining chocolate mixture. Smooth top. Freeze parfait overnight. (*Can be prepared 2 days ahead.*)

FOR SAUCE: Purée frozen boysenberries, sugar and crème de cassis in blender or processor until smooth. Strain. Add any berry purée reserved from parfait.

Unmold frozen parfait. Peel off plastic wrap. Slice into ½-inch-thick slices. Drizzle with sauce. Garnish with berries and fresh mint sprigs.

SPICED PUMPKIN PUDDING WITH WALNUT CREAM

This dessert is like a pumpkin pie without the crust, a fragrant custard baked in a pretty ceramic dish.

10 SERVINGS

3 cups half-and-half
6 large eggs
½ cup sugar
½ cup firmly packed golden brown sugar
6 tablespoons unsulfured (light) molasses
1½ teaspoons ground cinnamon
1½ teaspoons ground ginger
¾ teaspoon ground nutmeg
⅛ teaspoon (generous) ground cloves
¼ teaspoon salt
1½ 1-pound cans solid pack pumpkin
Walnut Cream (see recipe)

Preheat oven to 325°F. Butter shallow 8-cup baking dish. Bring half-and-half to simmer in small saucepan. Set aside. Beat eggs, both sugars, molasses, cinnamon, ginger, nutmeg, cloves and salt in large bowl to blend. Mix in pumpkin and warm half-and-half. Pour mixture into prepared dish. Set dish in large baking pan. Add enough hot water to pan to come halfway up sides of dish. Bake until custard is set and knife inserted 2 inches from center comes out clean, about 50 minutes. Cool completely. (*Can be prepared 1 day ahead. Cover and refrigerate.*) Serve cold or at room temperature with Walnut Cream.

WALNUT CREAM

10 SERVINGS

1½ cups chilled whipping cream
3 tablespoons powdered sugar
1½ tablespoons dark rum
¾ cup walnuts, toasted, finely chopped

Whip chilled cream in medium bowl until soft peaks form. Add powdered sugar and rum and whip until firm peaks form. Fold in chopped toasted walnuts. (*Can be prepared 4 hours ahead. Cover and chill.*)

PEACH-HONEY SMOOTHIE

2 SERVINGS

1¼ cups plain lowfat yogurt
1 pound ripe peaches, peeled, pitted, sliced
2 tablespoons fresh lemon juice
¼ cup honey
¼ teaspoon vanilla extract

Divide 1 cup yogurt among 8 sections of ice cube tray. Freeze until yogurt cubes are solid, at least 4 hours. (*Can be prepared 1 day ahead; keep frozen.*)

Purée peaches with lemon juice in processor or blender. Add remaining ¼ cup yogurt, honey and vanilla. Process until mixture is well blended. Add frozen yogurt cubes and process until mixture is smooth and frothy. Pour into chilled tall glasses and serve.

LIGHT DESSERTS

In the effort to maintain a wholesome diet, many people feel that they "blow it" on desserts. But ending a meal with a deliciously satisfying treat doesn't have to mean loading up on fat and calories. Instead, capitalize on dishes made with fruit, or try some of the many lowfat, no-cholesterol desserts now on the market. And, if you must, remember that moderation is the key. So just have a small slice of that marble fudge cheesecake.

Ripe fresh fruit—either puréed or diced—is a healthy replacement for fudge or butterscotch sauces.

If you have a recipe for a molded dessert or trifle that calls for pound cake, substitute angel food cake, which is lower in calories, fat and cholesterol.

In a muffin, coffee cake or chocolate cake recipe specifying sour cream, try yogurt as a healthful substitute.

Baste baked apples with apple cider for a simple, naturally sweet dessert.

A sophisticated and easy-to-prepare low-calorie dessert: peaches or pears poached in sweet wine, such as late harvest Riesling or Muscat.

Use sorbet or sherbet instead of ice cream for à la mode desserts.

Serve cookies that are made with egg whites, such as macaroons and meringues, instead of butter-rich treats.

LEMON SORBET WITH FRESH BLUEBERRIES AND BLUEBERRY SAUCE

8 SERVINGS

SAUCE

4 cups fresh blueberries or 1 pound
 frozen, thawed
1 cup water
3 tablespoons fresh lemon juice
2 tablespoons cornstarch
3 tablespoons sugar

3 half-pints lemon sorbet or
 sherbet
2 cups fresh blueberries

Thinly sliced lemon peel (yellow
part only)
Fresh lemon balm or mint sprigs
(garnish)

FOR SAUCE: Combine first 4 ingredients in heavy large saucepan. Stir over medium-high heat until mixture boils and thickens. Cool slightly. Purée mixture in processor or blender until smooth. Mix in sugar. Refrigerate until chilled, about 3 hours. (*Can be prepared 2 days ahead.*)

Scoop sorbet into goblets. Spoon sauce over. Top with fresh berries. Garnish with lemon peel and lemon balm.

BOYSENBERRY SORBET AND LEMON ICE CREAM BOMBE

12 SERVINGS

ICE CREAM

2¼ cups whipping cream
1 cup half-and-half
¾ cup sugar
6 egg yolks
½ cup fresh lemon juice
2 tablespoons finely grated lemon
 peel

SORBET

1¼ cups plus ⅓ cup sugar
¾ cup water

3 16-ounce bags frozen unsweetened
 boysenberries or blackberries,
 thawed

4 cups fresh boysenberries,
 blackberries and/or raspberries
 Fresh mint leaves (garnish)
 Assorted cookies (optional)

FOR ICE CREAM: Bring 1¼ cups cream, half-and-half and sugar to simmer in heavy large saucepan, stirring occasionally. Whisk yolks in large bowl to blend. Gradually whisk in cream mixture. Return mixture to saucepan. Stir over medium-low heat until mixture thickens and leaves path on back of spoon when finger is drawn across, about 4 minutes. Do not boil. Strain mixture into bowl. Mix in remaining 1 cup whipping cream, lemon juice and peel. Refrigerate until cold. Transfer mixture to ice cream maker and freeze according to manufacturer's instructions. Transfer ice cream to container and freeze.

FOR SORBET: Stir 1¼ cups sugar and

½ cup water in heavy medium saucepan over low heat until sugar dissolves. Purée 2 bags berries with sugar syrup in processor. Strain through coarse sieve into bowl, pressing firmly on seeds. Chill until cold. Transfer mixture to ice cream maker and freeze according to manufacturer's instructions.

Carefully line 12-cup ring mold with foil, pressing as smoothly as possible to eliminate wrinkles and extending over sides. Fill prepared ring mold alternately with ⅓-cup scoops sorbet and ⅓-cup scoops ice cream. Freeze 1 hour. Cover bombe with plastic. Press down firmly to pack. Freeze bombe overnight. *(Can be prepared 1 week ahead.)*

Purée remaining 1 bag of berries with remaining ⅓ cup sugar and ¼ cup water in processor. Strain through coarse sieve into bowl, pressing firmly on seeds. Cover sauce and chill until cold. *(Can be prepared 2 days ahead.)*

Place round platter in freezer 30 minutes. Lift bombe from mold using foil as aid. Invert bombe onto platter. Peel off foil. Mound some berries in center of bombe. Arrange more berries around sides. Garnish top and sides with mint. Cut into slices and arrange on plates. Spoon sauce and berries around each. Serve with cookies if desired.

DIABETES QUIZ

HEALTH AND NUTRITION ARE OF special concern to the 14 million Americans affected by diabetes. Unfortunately, nearly half don't realize they have the disorder. The American Diabetes Association has a quiz designed to alert you to symptoms if you think you might be at risk. For a free copy contact the ADA at 1660 Duke Street, Alexandria, VA 22314; 800-232-3472.

FOOD TIPS FOR TYKES

ANY PARENT KNOWS IT CAN BE tough teaching kids good eating habits. Not only do mom and dad have to please finicky youngsters, but they also have to interpret the latest food news, much of which does not address the special needs of children. One resource that does is *A Healthy Head Start* (Henry Holt and Company, 1990) by Mary Abbott Hess, M.S., R.D.; Anne Elise Hunt; and Barbara Motenko Stone. It's available in bookstores across the country.

HOW TO MAKE AN ICE CREAM BOMBE

For gala parties and special celebrations one of the most spec-tacular grand finales is the ice cream bombe—a rainbow of ice cream flavors and colors in a dome shape. Bombes involve successive layers of various flavors of ice cream arranged so that when sliced, each serving presents different bands of color. They can be made in ordinary mixing bowls. Here are some guidelines to be followed in creating the layers.

The bombe mold must be thoroughly chilled in the freezer before you line it with ice cream. If the mold is warmer than the ice cream, ice cream will slide down the sides.

To facilitate unmolding, brush inside of mold with unflavored oil and line with two strips of waxed paper about an inch wide crisscrossed at the bottom and extending over top.

Before constructing the bombe, allow the first ice cream to set in the freezer for at least two hours after it is churned to assure that it will be hard enough to pack.

The ice cream used in the outside layer, which is the support of the mold, must be one that hardens with age. Ice creams with sugar or liquor additions are unsuitable for the outside layer, although they are fine for the middle of the bombe.

The center of your bombe may be any ice cream, or for a more dramatic presentation, fill it with chopped nut brittle or chopped sweet chocolate, which will spill out attractively when the bombe is cut open for serving.

To launch you in the art of bombe making we suggest any of the following combinations:

Outer layer of vanilla, middle layer of mocha and a finely grated sweet chocolate center.

Outer layer of coffee, middle layer of vanilla, and a center of combined prune and Armagnac.

Outer layer of vanilla, middle layer of coffee-almond brittle, and a center of toasted almond bits.

continued on next page

HOW TO MAKE AN ICE CREAM BOMBE

Set aside a fourth of the outside ice cream to produce a "floor" when the bombe is inverted.

To ensure an absolutely even first layer, pack the ice cream firmly about 1½ inches thick onto the sides and bottom of the bowl. Then take another kitchen bowl the size of the cavity and place it in the empty space—pushing down gently to eliminate air pockets. Fill second bowl with ice cubes. This holds the walls while the ice cream hardens.

Keep the bombe frozen hard between periods of assembly.

When the first layer has frozen hard (probably the next day), pour a little hot water into the small support mixing bowl and twist it. It will slide out. Now pack in your second layer. Freeze again until hard.

To unmold, invert the frozen bombe onto a pre-chilled serving platter.

Dampen a kitchen towel with hot water and cover the outside of the mold. To encourage the mold to loosen, tug gently on the ends of the waxed paper ribbons. Immediately return the unmolded bombe to the freezer and, just before serving, garnish it with shaved chocolate, toasted slivered almonds, coconut, whipped cream rosettes, or whatever your imagination dictates.

CRANBERRY AND RASPBERRY STAR COOKIES

Perfect for the holiday season. Cranberries add tang to the filling of these colorful sandwich cookies. You will have some small unsandwiched cookies, too.

MAKES ABOUT
36 SANDWICH COOKIES

COOKIES

¾ cup (1½ sticks) unsalted butter, room temperature
1 teaspoon vanilla extract
¼ teaspoon grated lemon peel
1 cup sugar
1 large egg
1 egg yolk
2¼ cups all purpose flour
¼ cup cornstarch
¼ teaspoon (generous) ground cloves

FILLING

1 cup fresh cranberries
¼ cup sugar

¾ cup raspberry preserves

Powdered sugar

FOR COOKIES: Using electric mixer, cream butter, vanilla and lemon in bowl until light. Gradually add sugar and beat until blended. Beat in egg and yolk. Combine flour, cornstarch and cloves. Beat half of dry ingredients into butter mixture. Stir in remaining dry ingredients. Gather dough into ball. Divide dough into 4 pieces; flatten each into disk. Wrap each in plastic and chill 1 hour.

Preheat oven to 350°F. Butter heavy large nonstick cookie sheets. Roll 1 dough piece out (keep remainder refrigerated) on floured surface to thickness of ⅛ inch. Cut out star-shaped cookies using floured 3-inch star cutter. Transfer to prepared cookie sheets, spacing ½ inch apart. Repeat rolling and cutting with second dough piece. Gather scraps and reroll, chilling dough briefly if soft. Cut out more 3-inch star cookies. Transfer to prepared cookie sheets. Chill cookies 10 minutes. Bake until edges are golden, about 10 minutes. Cool on rack.

Roll third dough piece out on lightly floured surface to thickness of ⅛ inch. Cut out star-shaped cookies using floured 3-inch star cutter. Cut smaller star out of center of each 3-inch star using 1¾- to 2-inch star cutter. Transfer star outlines to prepared cookie sheets using floured metal spatula as aid. Repeat rolling and cutting star outlines with fourth dough piece. Gather scraps and star centers and reroll, chilling dough briefly if soft. Cut out 3-inch stars. Cut smaller stars out of each 3-inch star. Transfer star outlines and centers to prepared cookie sheets. Chill cookies 10 minutes. Bake until edges are golden brown, about 9 minutes. Transfer cookies to rack and cool.

FOR FILLING: Finely chop cranberries with sugar in processor. Transfer mixture to heavy medium saucepan. Mix in preserves. Cook over medium-high heat until mixture is reduced to scant 1 cup, stirring occasionally, about 8 minutes.

Pour into bowl and cool.

Using metal icing spatula, spread 1 teaspoon jam filling in center of each 3-inch cookie, spreading slightly toward points of star. Lightly sift powdered sugar over star outlines. Place star outlines sugar side up over jam-topped cookies. (*Can be prepared ahead. Place in single layers in airtight containers. Refrigerate up to 4 days or freeze up to 2 weeks. Let stand 10 minutes at room temperature before serving.*)

A WORLD OF COFFEE

As with most things in life, the best coffee is the one you like best. And the only way to discover which particular bean that may be is to sample a few different kinds.

Here is some general information about the characteristics of the best exports from a few famous coffee-producing countries. Remember, no two coffee beans from the same country are the same; location, climate, picking, processing, transportation, storage and roasting all make a difference.

Colombia: Heavy body, aromatic, balanced acidity, mild taste, winy. Best-known blend is Medellín.

Costa Rica: Medium body, very aromatic, good acidity, winy.

Guatemala: Full body, very winy, wonderful bouquet. Best-known are Antigua and Cobán.

Hawaii: Known as Kona. Light body, mild winyness, slightly nutty.

Indonesia: Sumatran is dry, smooth and full-bodied. Java variety is rich, full-bodied and winy with a spicy, smoky fragrance and mature flavor. Often mixed with Yemeni Mocha beans.

Kenya: Full body, aromatic bouquet, very winy flavors.

Tanzania: Sharp, extremely winy, medium to full-bodied.

LEMON-ANISE PIROUETTES

Enjoy the crisp, delicate treats on their own or with ice cream or mousse.

MAKES ABOUT 60

½ cup sugar
¼ cup powdered sugar
 2 teaspoons grated lemon peel
 1 teaspoon aniseed, finely chopped
½ teaspoon fennel seeds, finely chopped
 6 tablespoons (¾ stick) unsalted butter, room temperature
 3 large egg whites, room temperature
½ teaspoon vanilla extract
½ cup all purpose flour

Position rack in center of oven and preheat to 350°F. Lightly butter large non-stick cookie sheet. Blend first 5 ingredients in processor 1 minute. Using electric mixer, cream butter in medium bowl until light. Gradually beat in sugar mixture, egg whites and vanilla. Add flour and beat until combined.

Drop 1 teaspoon batter onto prepared cookie sheet. Using back of spoon, spread into 3-inch round. Repeat 5 more times, spacing cookies evenly. Bake until cookies are golden brown on edges, about 5 minutes.

Immediately run tip of small knife under edge of 1 cookie. Using fingertips, pick up cookie at lifted edge and turn over onto work surface. Working quickly, roll cookie around handle of wooden spoon, pressing cookie against handle as you roll. Slide cookie off handle. Repeat rolling with remaining cookies on sheet, returning sheet briefly to oven if cookies begin to harden.

Rinse cookie sheet under cold water. Dry with towel. Lightly butter cookie sheet. Repeat making cookies with remaining batter in batches, rinsing, drying and buttering sheet between each batch. Cool cookies. (*Can be prepared 2 weeks ahead. Transfer to airtight container; store at room temperature.*)

BEST OF BOTH WORLDS

EACH OF THE 150 TEMPTING RECIPES in *Lean or Lavish* by Judith Pacht (Warner Books, 1991) has two exciting versions to choose from—one for when you need to count calories and another for when a little indulgence is in order. Nutritional data follow each recipe to help you weigh your options. Tips on menu planning are included, and wine suggestions from Hank Rubin, longtime wine columnist for *Bon Appétit,* round out the book.

Fig and Walnut Truffles

MAKES 36

¾ cup whipping cream
6 tablespoons (¾ stick) unsalted
   butter
3 tablespoons light corn syrup
12 ounces semisweet chocolate
   (such as Baker's), chopped
1 tablespoon Cognac or other
   brandy
⅔ cup chopped dried Calimyrna figs
⅔ cup choppped toasted walnuts

Unsweetened cocoa powder

Heat cream, unsalted butter and corn syrup in heavy medium saucepan over medium heat until just boiling, stirring occasionally. Remove saucepan from heat, add semisweet chocolate to cream mixture and stir until chocolate melts and mixture is smooth. Mix in Cognac. Add figs and walnuts and blend well. Spoon mixture into 8x8-inch glass dish with 2-inch-high sides. Cover and refrigerate until mixture is firm enough to handle, about 1 hour.

Cut chocolate mixture into 36 squares. Roll each square by hand to form round. Dust rounds lightly with cocoa. Place truffles in foil-lined dish. Cover and chill until firm, at least 4 hours. (*Can be prepared 4 days ahead.*)

Hazelnut Thumbprint Cookies

This recipe doubles easily. Fill half the cookies with orange marmalade and the other half with raspberry preserves for a nice flavor selection.

MAKES ABOUT 2 DOZEN

1 cup sifted all purpose flour
⅛ teaspoon salt
½ cup (1 stick) unsalted butter,
   room temperature
⅓ cup sugar
1 egg yolk
¾ teaspoon vanilla extract
¼ cup toasted hazelnuts, coarsely
   ground (about 4 ounces)

**Orange marmalade and/or
raspberry preserves**

Preheat oven to 350°F. Combine flour and salt in small bowl. Using electric mixer, cream butter in large bowl until fluffy. Add sugar and beat until light and fluffy. Mix in yolk and vanilla. Mix in dry ingredients and nuts.

Form dough into 1-inch balls. Arrange on ungreased cookie sheet, spacing 1½ inches apart. Make depression in center of each using fingertip or handle of wooden spoon. Bake 10 minutes. Fill depressions with marmalade and/or preserves. Continues baking until cookies begin to color, about 10 minutes. Cool on rack. Store airtight.

CARROT ORANGE COOKIES

These cakelike cookies are a good use for leftover carrots: Your kids will never know!

MAKES ABOUT 30

10 ounces carrots, sliced

¾ cup solid vegetable shortening
¾ cup sugar
1 egg, beaten to blend
1 teaspoon vanilla extract
2 cups all purpose flour
1 teaspoon baking powder
½ teaspoon salt
⅔ cup chopped walnuts

1 cup powdered sugar
2 tablespoons orange juice
¼ teaspoon grated orange peel

Cook carrots in saucepan of boiling water until tender, about 15 minutes. Drain well. Puree in processor. (You should have about 1 cup.)

Preheat oven to 350°F. Grease cookie sheets. Beat shortening with sugar. Mix in egg. Stir in vanilla. Combine flour, baking powder and salt. Stir dry ingredients into butter mixture alternately with carrot puree. Mix in walnuts. Drop by rounded tablespoonfuls onto prepared cookie sheets. Bake until light brown and springy to touch, about 20 minutes.

Stir together remaining ingredients until smooth. Spread atop warm cookies. (*Can be prepared 1 day ahead. Store in airtight container.*)

TOFFEE CRUNCH FANS

Chopped toffee candy is folded into a classic shortbread dough, which is patted out into a round and scored into fans.

MAKES 12

¾ cup (1½ sticks) unsalted butter, room temperature
⅓ cup packed dark brown sugar

¾ teaspoon vanilla extract
1½ cups all purpose flour
¼ cup cornstarch
¼ teaspoon salt
2 1.2-ounce packages chocolate-covered English toffee bars (such as Heath Bars), chopped

Preheat oven to 350°F. Using electric mixer, cream butter until light. Add brown sugar and vanilla and beat until light and fluffy. Combine flour, cornstarch and salt. Add to butter and mix until beginning to gather together. Mix in chopped toffee bars.

Grease 10-inch glass pie dish. Press dough into bottom of pie dish, building edges ½ inch up sides. Use fork to crimp edges. Cut into 12 wedges, using ruler as guide and cutting all the way through dough. Pierce each wedge 3 times with fork. Bake until barely firm to touch and beginning to color, about 30 minutes. Recut wedges. Cool in pie dish on rack. (*Store in airtight container.*)

INDEX

ACKNOWLEDGEMENTS & CREDITS

Recipes and text supplied by:

Melanie Barnard
Sarah Belk
Kathryn and Anthony Dias Blue
Georgeanne Brennan
Charleen Borger
Anne Boulard
Russell Cronkhite
Lane S. Crowther
William Detraz
Brooke Dojny
Sue Ellison
Ellen Faris

Jim Fobel
Vené Franco
Harris Golden
Marcy Goldman
Leslie Holliday
Karen A. Kaplan
Jeanne Thiel Kelley
Kristine Kidd
Elinor Klivans
Jacqueline Lauby
Nadia Marmach
Lori A. McKean

Michael McLaughlin
Jinx and Jefferson Morgan
Selma Brown Morrow
Eleanor Moscatel
Steven Raichlen
Betty Rosbottom
John Salisbury
Richard Sax
Michele Sbrana
Lori D. Shaller
Ilana Sharlin
Marie Simmons

Kristin H.R. Small
Dorothy Smith
Suzanne Solberg
Marlene Spieler
Ana St. Amand
Sandy Swarc
Sarah Tenaglia
Tarla Thiel
Cynthia Paige Ward
Kate Zentall

Concept:
Susan M. Allyn

Editorial development and original writing:
Norman Kolpas

Graphic design:
Sandy Douglas

Illustrations:
Michelle Burchard

Production:
Joan Valentine

Index:
Barbara Wurf

Proofreader:
Katie Goldman

Rights and permissions:
Gaylen Ducker Grody